LEARNING TO DRIVE A TRUCK

Údarás Um Shábháilteacht Ar Bhóithre
Road Safety Authority

First published by Údarás Um Shábháilteacht Ar Bhóithre / Road Safety Authority 2012

© 2012 Údarás Um Shábháilteacht Ar Bhóithre / Road Safety Authority

ISBN 978-0-9567931-2-6

10 9 8 7 6 5 4 3 2 1

Údarás Um Shábháilteacht Ar Bhóithre
Road Safety Authority

Páirc Ghnó Ghleann na Muaidhe, Cnoc an tSabhaircín,
Bóthar Bhaile Átha Cliath, Béal an Átha, Co. Mhaigh Eo.

Moy Valley Business Park, Primrose Hill, Dublin Road, Ballina, Co. Mayo.

locall: 1890 50 60 80   fax: (096) 25 252
email: info@rsa.ie   website: www.rsa.ie

Every effort has been made to ensure the accuracy and reliability of information contained in this book. The Road Safety Authority cannot accept responsibility for any inaccuracies or errors, and any reliance that readers place in this book or in the information contained in it is at their own risk. Information in this book is for guidance only.

In no event will the Road Safety Authority be liable for any loss or damage, including without limitation, indirect or consequential loss or damage, or any loss or damage whatsoever arising out of, or in connection with the use of this book.

Foreword

Building a strong safety culture on Irish roads is the core mission of the RSA, one that is centred very firmly on drivers and their behaviour on the road.

Research from all around the world tells us that the manner in which people learn to drive is a key factor in their future behaviour on the road – they are more likely to be safe and competent behind the wheel when they have learned within a staged and formal process, and where they have taken responsibility for their own learning experience.

The purpose of this book is help learner truck drivers to do just that – and to place what you learn with your Approved Driving Instructor within a broader context where you are taking responsibility.

The sheer size, weight and power of trucks makes driving one very different from driving a car or a van; and a key element in becoming a safe and competent truck driver is to understand the vulnerability of other road users, especially cyclists and pedestrians.

Being able to drive a truck is a very valuable social and economic asset, and for most people it opens up potential for good employment in a variety of industries.

We are confident that this book can make a contribution to continuing the improvement in Irish road safety. We wish all learner truck drivers many years of safe driving.

Noel Brett, Chief Executive Officer, RSA

Contents

1. Becoming a truck driver 9
   - Assessing your progress 9
   - Truck driving licences 10
   - The learner driver and the law 11
   - What is the Driver CPC? 12
   - Things to know and things to do 14
   - Choosing an ADI 15
   - Programme of learning 16

2. Before you start 17
   - Basic truck maintenance knowledge 17
   - Know your truck – before you turn on the engine 19
   - Your daily walk-around check 22
   - Minding your load 27
   - Route planning 28

3. Gaining experience on the road 30
   - Starting and stopping the truck: the first time 30
   - Your first time on the road 33
   - Planning practice journeys 35
   - Reading the road 35
   - Knowing your position on the road 36
   - Dealing with junctions 37
   - Controlling your speed 45
   - Signalling your intentions 46
   - Reversing 48
   - Parking 50
   - Coupling and uncoupling a trailer 50
   - Overtaking 52
   - Starting on a hill 53
   - Preparing for the unexpected 54
   - Driving on motorways 54

4. Complying with regulations 57
- Drivers' hours 57
- How much rest to take 61
- Tachographs 63
- Certificate of Roadworthiness 64
- Road Haulage Operator's Licence 65
- Carrying hazardous materials 66
- Wide and abnormal loads 67

5. Dealing with more challenging conditions 69
- Dealing with hazards 69
- Driving in heavy traffic 70
- Night-time driving 71
- Driving in conditions of poor visibility 73
- Driving in poor on-road conditions 76
- Driving in high winds 78
- Dealing with road works and other obstructions 79
- Town and country: challenges of urban and rural driving 80

6. Sharing the road 83
- Making sure you're fit to drive 83
- Staying calm: showing courtesy 86
- Avoiding and dealing with distractions while driving 87
- Dealing with other road users 88
- Thinking of the environment 92
- Dealing with collisions and emergencies 94
- Dealing with a breakdown 95

Summary of commitments 97

Using this book

Almost all of the items that we eat and drink, all the furniture that we sit on and sleep in, all the clothes we wear have all spent some part of their lives in a truck. Even the cars we drive at some point were delivered to a garage on a vehicle transporter. For that reason, there is great variety in truck driving, and in the course of a career you could find yourself transporting building materials, foodstuffs, bulk liquids, waste materials, live animals and so on.

For most people, learning to drive a truck is not just about learning to drive a bigger vehicle, it's also about learning to become a professional driver, someone who will make their livelihood from driving.

You will use the same well-developed skills of observation and anticipation that you use when driving a car, but more acutely and well in advance. As someone who will be driving for a living, you need to learn to behave in a responsible and professional manner at all times.

Chapter by chapter

The purpose of this book is to help you to take responsibility for your own learning as a truck driver. It presents a typical path that you might follow as a learner truck driver.

Chapter 1. Becoming a truck driver: this chapter describes the steps you need to take to become a professional truck driver. This includes some of the legal issues around driving a truck, the various theory and practical tests you need to take, and the importance of the Certificate of Professional Competence (CPC).

Chapter 2. Before you start: this chapter covers the skills and knowledge you need to have before you begin to drive a truck. This includes knowledge of all the truck's controls and how to do basic maintenance and safety checks.

Chapter 3. Gaining experience on the road: this chapter focuses on the skills you need to master, including starting and stopping, changing gears, keeping up with traffic, knowing your position on the road, and dealing with junctions of all kinds. It also covers manoeuvres such as reversing, parking, starting on hills, and coupling and uncoupling a trailer.

Chapter 4. Complying with regulations: this chapter deals with some of the many regulations that truck drivers have to comply with. These include regulations relating to drivers' hours and tachographs, obtaining a Certificate of Roadworthiness and a Haulage Operator's Licence, the carriage of dangerous materials, and the transport of wide or abnormal loads.

Chapter 5. Dealing with more challenging conditions: this chapter takes what you've learned in chapter 3 and applies it to more difficult or challenging conditions – including bad weather, driving at night, driving in heavy traffic and driving on different types of road.

Chapter 6. Sharing the road: this chapter looks at some of the personal qualities you need to develop to become a consistently safe and competent truck driver. These include qualities such as being able to stay calm under pressure, to treat other road users with courtesy and respect, and to commit yourself to driving only when you are physically and mentally fit to do so safely. It also looks at things you can do to reduce the impact of your driving on the environment. Lastly it gives some tips on what to do if you are the first person at the scene of a collision.

1. Becoming a truck driver

In this chapter

This chapter describes the steps you need to take to become a truck driver. Most people who learn how to drive a truck do so because they want to drive professionally, and to do this they need to have:

- A truck driving licence; and
- A Driver CPC (certificate of professional competence).

In order to get these qualifications you will need to set out on a course of study and of practice, and the best way to do this is to work with an Approved Driving Instructor (ADI).

This chapter also describes the periodic training that you need to do in order to keep up your professional qualification.

Assessing your progress

When you learn to drive a truck, you learn to take responsibility. This includes taking responsibility for keeping track of your own learning and being honest with yourself about the progress you are making.

Throughout this book there are '**My commitment**' panels where you are invited to sign off on areas of competence or knowledge that you have mastered. These cover most of the theory, practice and good habits that you need to learn in order to become a safe and competent truck driver. By signing off on these commitments, you are affirming that:

- You have mastered a particular area of competence or knowledge;
- You understand the risks and hazards relating to that competence; and
- You are making a commitment about your own behaviour as a truck driver.

When you are confident that you have arrived at a satisfactory level of competence in a particular knowledge or theory area, you can 'sign off' on that area. That amounts to you saying 'Yes, I'm confident that I ...'. **Don't sign off on an area until you're fully confident**. If you feel you're close but not quite there on a particular area, ask your ADI for advice.

# Truck driving licences

The category of driving licence you need depends on what kind of truck you want to drive, as shown in the following table.

Vehicle	Description	Category
	Vehicles (other than motorcycles, mopeds, work vehicles or land tractors) with: ○ a design gross vehicle weight of 3,500 kg or less, and seating for up to 8 passengers (apart from the driver). These include a trailer when the trailer's design gross vehicle weight is 750 kg or less.	B
	Vehicles in category C with a design gross vehicle weight of 7,500 kg or less. These include a trailer when the trailer's design gross vehicle weight is 750 kg or less.	C1
	Vehicles (other than work vehicles or land tractors) with: ○ a design gross vehicle weight of more than 3,500 kg, and seating for up to 8 passengers (apart from the driver). These include a trailer when the trailer's design gross vehicle weight is 750 kg or less.	C
	Combinations of vehicles and trailers when: ○ the towing vehicle in category C1 and the trailer have a combined design gross vehicle weight of 12,000 kg or less, and ○ the design gross vehicle weight of the trailer does not exceed the unladen weight of the drawing vehicle.	EC1
	Combinations of vehicles and trailers when: ○ the towing vehicle is in category C; and ○ the trailer's design gross vehicle weight is greater than 750 kg and includes an articulated unit.	EC

For each licence category there is an equivalent learner permit.

Getting your learner permit

You need a learner permit for the type of truck that you want to learn to drive. Application forms for learner permits (D 201) and medical report forms (D 501) are available at Garda stations, at local Motor Tax offices and at Driving Test Centres.

- You must be 18 years at least to apply for a truck learner permit, and you must be normally resident in Ireland.
- If this is your first time applying for a truck learner permit, you must apply for and pass the truck driver theory test.
- The first time you apply for any truck learner permit you must supply a satisfactory medical report completed by a doctor on form D 501.

What you need to get a truck learner permit

The following table summarises what category of licence you need in order to apply for each category of truck learner permit.

To apply for …	You need to already hold:
… a **C1** learner permit	… a **B** licence
… a **C** learner permit	… a **B** licence *or* a **C1** licence
… an **EC1** learner permit	… a **C** licence *or* a **C1** licence
… an **EC** learner permit	… a **C** licence

The truck driver theory test – before you get a learner permit

Before you apply for your first truck learner permit, you must do a truck driver theory test. This test is similar in design and format to the driver theory test you do to get your car learner permit.

The learner driver and the law

Before you drive a truck on the public road, you need to make sure that you are legal in every way:

- You must be insured to drive the vehicle as a learner;
- The vehicle must be taxed and insured;
- The vehicle must be roadworthy and it must have a current Certificate of Road Worthiness;
- You must carry an up-to-date truck learner permit at all times while you are driving a truck – see **Getting your learner permit** above;

- While you are learning you must be accompanied at all times by a suitably qualified driver who has had a full licence for at least two years in the category of vehicle you are driving;
- Your vehicle must display regulation L-plates (front and rear) at all times while you are driving; and
- While you are a truck driver learner permit holder, you may not drive a truck on a motorway.

What is the Driver CPC?

The Driver CPC (Certificate of Professional Competence) is an EU-wide qualification that sets high standards for professional driver competence across Europe. The main aims of the Driver CPC are:

- To make sure that all professional drivers have good driving and safety standards and that they keep up those standards throughout their careers;
- To create a common standard for the training and testing of drivers throughout the EU; and
- To help reduce fatalities and serious injuries.

If you wish to work as a professional truck driver, you need both a truck driving licence for the category of truck you will be driving and a Driver CPC.

The steps to becoming a professional truck driver

Before you apply for a Driver CPC, you must have a full category B licence and you must have passed the truck driver theory test (and have a truck driver learner permit). You can then proceed to the four Driver CPC tests.

Test 1	A two-hour multiple-choice theory test	This test consists of 100 multiple-choice questions. You need to answer at least 61 correctly in order to pass.	These theory tests are carried out by Prometric Ireland on behalf of the RSA. Most applicants would sit these tests on the same day.
Test 2	A two-hour case study theory test	This test consists of three case studies describing various scenarios that a driver might face. In each case study there are 15 questions (45 in total). To pass you need to answer at least 5 questions correctly from each case study and at least 28 in total.	

When you have passed the two Driver CPC theory tests you can then apply to sit the practical tests.

Test 3	A 90-minute practical truck driving test	This is a standard truck driving test for the category of licence you are applying for – C, C1, EC1 or EC.
Test 4	A 30-minute practical knowledge test	The purpose of this test is to check your knowledge of your vehicle and how to operate it safely and effectively. You will be asked questions on areas such as safety, legal matters relating to driving, vehicle loading and stability, physical risks involved in driving, and what to do in an emergency.

For non-professional truck drivers

If you do not intend working as a professional truck driver, you are not required to have a Driver CPC – you can apply to sit the standard truck driving test (Test 3 above) without first passing the Driver CPC theory tests.

The order in which you do your CPC and driving tests

The first practical driving test that you can sit is a category C or C1 test, and most truck learner drivers would sit one of these on the same day as the CPC practical knowledge test. Once you have a category C1 or C licence, you can do the category EC or EC1 test at a later stage.

Once you have passed the Truck Driver CPC once, you don't have to do it again. You do, however, have to keep your Truck Driver CPC up to date – see Driver CPC: periodic training to keep up your skills on page 14.

Even with a Driver CPC you are entitled to drive only those vehicles covered by your driving licence. In other words, a driver with a Driver CPC and a C licence may legally drive vehicles in category C and C1 but may not legally drive a vehicle in category EC.

Tachographs and the Digital Tachograph Driver Card

To work as a professional truck driver, you may need to use a tachograph – see page 63 for more information about tachographs.

Driver CPC: periodic training to keep up your skills

CPC periodic training is training you need to do every year to keep up your Driver CPC. All professional truck drivers must complete the five Periodic Training courses over a period of five years – that is, one seven-hour course per year. The learning areas covered are:

- Control of Vehicle and Eco Driving Techniques
- Minimising Risks and Managing Emergencies in the Transport Industry
- The Professional Truck Driver*
- Health and Safety of the Professional Driver
- Role of the Professional Driver in the Transport Industry
- The Professional Bus Driver*

* If you are a professional truck and bus driver, you need to cover all six of these areas within five years.

CPC Periodic Training will help you improve your knowledge and skills so that you remain a driver of the highest professional standard. It will also help you to keep up to date with changes in the industry.

See the RSA's website for more information on Driver CPC – see under **Professional Drivers**.

Things to know and things to do

The best way to acquire the required knowledge and to develop the right skills and habits is to work with an Approved Driving Instructor (ADI) throughout the time you are learning. Driving a truck has much in common with driving a car, but there are also many differences.

To become a safe and competent truck driver, there are things you need to know and things you need to do. You need to acquire knowledge and develop skills.

Things you need to know: acquire knowledge

The things you need to know include:

- Rules and regulations, including the *Rules of the Road*;
- Basic concepts about how the truck works, including: knowledge of the gears and transmission system and the braking system;
- How to manage your vehicle – this includes load restraint, loading and unloading, and other skills depending on the particular type of vehicle you are driving; and
- Basic preventative maintenance and routine safety checks.

Things you need to do: develop skills

The things you need to do include:

- Planning your learning, setting yourself goals, and monitoring your progress;
- Practising your truck driving skills within a structured programme;
- Learning techniques for safe and fuel-efficient driving; and
- Observing road usage and developing your skills of judgement.

Choosing an ADI

Learning to drive a truck is a very challenging task, and the best way to do this is to follow a course of instruction from an RSA-registered Approved Driving Instructor (ADI). Among the many benefits from doing this:

- You don't have to have your own truck;
- Trucks provided by ADIs for learner training are fitted with dual controls; and
- You can call upon all the experience and knowledge of the ADI while you are learning.

Your ADI

Anyone who accepts payment for teaching you to drive must be on the RSA's Register of Approved Driving Instructors (ADI) and display an Approved Driving Instructor permit. To become registered and get an ADI full permit, each instructor is assessed by the RSA. They are required to have:

- Knowledge of the *Rules of the Road* and road safety;
- Driving ability; and
- Ability to teach a learner driver.

Your ADI is the expert to whom you should direct any questions that you have about driving. ADIs who specialise in trucks usually have a wealth of experience and knowledge about driving trucks and they know how to pass on their expertise to learner truck drivers.

For your protection, ADIs also undergo Garda vetting. What this means for you, as a learner driver, is better, more consistent standards and therefore better instruction. The RSA Register lists ADIs around the country, together with their contact details and the category or categories of vehicle in which they can provide instruction – see the RSA website at www.rsa.ie.

Make sure that the driving school or instructor you choose is registered with the RSA for instructing drivers in the relevant category of vehicle, and that it has the vehicles, facilities and instructors that you need to help you learn to drive a truck.

 An accompanying driver may not accept payment for helping you to learn to drive a truck, unless they are a registered ADI.

Údarás Um Shábháilteacht Ar Bhóithre
Road Safety Authority

My commitment 1
I understand the responsibility of taking a truck onto the road and of sharing the road with other people. I am ready to take on that personal responsibility and to take ownership of how I learn how to drive a truck.
Signed (Learner)

Programme of learning

The things you learn and the things you do go hand in hand and influence each other. The theory you learn informs how you drive; and your driving practice makes sense of the theory you have learnt. Using the theory and practice together help you to develop the good habits of safe and competent driving.

Your ADI will guide you through a programme of learning that includes both the knowledge you need to gain and the practical skills you need to develop.

You should first master the basic skills of controlling the truck at low speed in a very safe traffic-free place – for example, an empty car park. Wait until you are comfortable controlling the truck before going any further and before taking the truck onto the public road.

The first time you drive on the public road should be in very light traffic conditions and on roads that afford good visibility. As you become more skilled and have more confidence behind the wheel, you need to practise in more challenging conditions.

2. Before you start

In this chapter

This chapter outlines the skills and knowledge you need before you begin to drive a truck.

- Basic truck maintenance knowledge: you need to have this before you learn to drive. It is an essential part of your responsibility as a driver to make sure that your truck is safe and roadworthy.
- Getting to know your truck: you also need to get familiar with all of the truck's controls, in particular the gears and brakes. You need to know where they are and how to operate them. You also need to know your truck's weights and dimensions.
- Your daily walk-around check: a professional truck driver carries out a detailed safety check of the vehicle every day before taking it on the road. Typically, this covers external checks, in-cab checks, pre-departure checks, and checks that you do when you are on the road.
- Minding your load: you are responsible for ensuring that your cargo is correctly and safely loaded.

Basic truck maintenance knowledge

You are responsible for making sure that the truck you drive is in a safe and roadworthy condition. So, you need to know something about basic maintenance. You are about to learn how to control a very powerful and potentially dangerous piece of equipment. In particular, you need to make sure that you have enough fuel, that your tyres are correctly inflated and that your lights are working correctly.

Familiarise yourself with the truck's user manual or handbook. Ask your ADI to give you a 'guided tour' of the basic truck maintenance tasks that you need to perform. See page 22 for details of the daily walk-around check that every professional truck driver needs to carry out.

Fuel

The one basic maintenance task that you will have do regularly is to put the correct fuel in your truck. Not all service stations are designed with the needs of truck drivers in mind. So before you enter a service station, check that the forecourt roof is not too low for your truck and you can manoeuvre it up to the diesel pump.

Tyres

Well-maintained tyres are essential for safe, economical driving.

Tyre pressure	There is wide variation in the recommended tyre pressure for different kinds of truck, so you should always follow the manufacturer's specifications for tyre pressure – check the truck's handbook.
Tyre condition	Well-maintained tyres are essential for safety. Check the tyres for any visible defects such as bubbles or blistering in the tyre walls or any other visible defects.
Tyre tread depth	Tyres should have the minimum legal tread depth of 1.6mm.

Checking the oil

Engine oil plays an essential role in keeping your engine lubricated and running smoothly. You should check the oil level regularly (in line with the manufacturer's recommendations) and top up if necessary. On some modern trucks, the oil level is monitored automatically via a dashboard display.

Depending on what truck you have, you might also need to check separately the gearbox oil and the transmission oil. See your truck's handbook for details of the recommended grades of oil and the oil levels, and how often you should check them.

Radiator fluid

The radiator contains a fluid that helps to cool the engine and prevent corrosion. Check the coolant fluid while the engine is cold. The radiator is usually accessible via the front grille. In most vehicles there is a minimum marker that the coolant should cover. If necessary, top up with the coolant recommended by your truck's handbook.

When to call in the experts

Before you bring a truck onto the public road you need to be sure that it is safe in every respect. In addition to your detailed daily walk-around checks (see page 22), you need to be able to identify other defects that could compromise the safety of your vehicle. For example, the braking, power steering and electrical systems must all be in perfect working order, and a fault as simple as a leak from the power steering system could make the truck much more difficult to control and manoeuvre. Modern truck engines and controls are very complex and they should be maintained by suitably qualified mechanics only.

In your first few minutes driving you should be able to assess how the truck is handling on the road. If you suspect that there are any serious defects, pull in at a safe place and follow your company's safety procedures or policy guidelines.

Know your truck – before you turn on the engine

Before you turn on the engine and begin to drive a truck, there are a few things you need to know and a few things you need to be able to do. These include making yourself comfortable, getting to know all the controls, and adjusting your mirrors for maximum visibility.

Entering and leaving the truck

Each time you enter or leave a truck cab, you need to make sure that it is safe to do so. A cab door opening can be a hazard to passing traffic, particularly to cyclists. Always face the truck as you enter or leave the cab, and use the steps and rails provided. Never jump from the vehicle.

Make yourself comfortable

When you sit in the driver's seat of a truck, you need to make sure that the seat is comfortable, that the seatbelt is working correctly, that the head restraint is correctly adjusted, and that the steering wheel is adjusted for your comfort and safety.

Driver's seat	Adjust the driver's seat so that you are comfortable, have good visibility, and can reach the pedals and all the hand controls easily. The driver's seat can usually be moved up and down and back and forth, and you can also adjust the angle of the back of the seat.
Steering wheel	Most modern trucks have steering wheels that you can adjust to your comfort and safety. The controls vary depending on the make and model of the truck. Ask your ADI to help you with the adjustment – you need to make sure that you can turn the steering wheel easily without causing any strain to your back, shoulders or arms.

Know your dashboard controls

Check that you know where all the controls and dials are. If this is your first time in a truck, you will notice quite a few controls that cars don't have. Depending on the truck, these could include air pressure dials, a lift axles button and so on. Again, ask your ADI to give you a guided tour of all the controls.

Adjust your mirrors

Adjust all your mirrors, including the wide angle and 'cyclops' mirrors so that they are all angled correctly from your viewing position.

The gears

As a car driver you're probably used to five forward gears and reverse. When you sit into a truck, you quickly realise that it's a bit more complicated, with some larger trucks having up to twenty-four forward gears.

In most trucks, gears are split between low ratio and high ratio gears, the most common arrangement being 'four over four' to give eight forward gears. Where there are more than six gears, the gear stick usually has a switch to enable you to change between low and high ratios.

There is considerable variation in the arrangement and positioning of gears in trucks, and different makes of truck have different systems including some automatic and semi-automatic gearboxes. Ask your ADI to demonstrate the gear changing on the truck you are in.

The brakes

Most trucks have three different brakes: the standard foot brake and parking brake that you are familiar with from driving a car and (in addition) a retarder / exhaust brake:

Standard brakes	The foot brake (sometimes referred to as the service brake) and the parking brake work in the same way as they do in a car.
Retarder / exhaust brake	Use the retarder / exhaust brake to reduce speed without using the standard brakes – for example when you are coming down a steep hill. (Note that your brake lights may be activated when you use the retarder.)
	Ask your ADI to show you when and how to use the retarder or exhaust brake.

How long, how wide, how high, how heavy

When you are driving a truck on the public road, you need to develop an understanding and awareness of where you are on the road in relation to other vehicles, to street furniture (such as bollards, lamp posts and so on) and to other objects – including road signs, overhanging trees, traffic islands and so on. Coming to terms with the size of the particular truck you are driving is essential.

Within category C, trucks can vary considerably in length, height and weight. And if you are driving a category EC truck, there's an even wider range.

Your truck must have a Vehicle Weights and Dimensions Plate detailing its length, height, width and weight (on each axle).

If you have a trailer, it should also have a Vehicle Weights and Dimensions Plate.

Length and width

Knowing the length and width of your truck will help you when it comes to manoeuvring in a tight space – for example, when you are parking, emerging from an exit or reversing into a loading bay. You also need to be sure that the whole vehicle can proceed through a yellow box junction – this is particularly important at railway level crossings.

Height

If the overall height of the truck is over 3 metres, then you must display a height indicator prominently inside the cab.

Bridges over 5.03 metres (16ft 6in) are not usually marked, as this is considered high enough for road vehicles. The clearance height on low bridges is indicated by an advance sign and also on the bridge itself in both metres and feet and inches. Some arch-shaped bridges have lower clearance to the side, so keep to the centre as you pass under them – if necessary, wait for a gap in traffic.

See also

Iarnród Éireann has a page on its website dedicated to bridge heights, so if you plan to travel on a route with a low bridge, check the height in advance.

www.irishrail.ie/bridgeheights/bridge_heights.asp

If you do strike a bridge, you are legally required to report it. Bridges with restricted headroom display a rectangular plate that identifies the bridge number and also shows the phone number to call in the event of a collision.

Weight

You also need to know details about the weight of your truck, and the weight bearing on each axle.

The unladen weight	The weight of the truck not including fuel, water, the driver or any cargo.
Design GVW (gross vehicle weight)	The maximum or gross design vehicle weight, including the load, fuel, water, the driver and so on.
Weight of load	The weight of the load you are carrying – how you determine this will depend on the load. For loose material such as sand or gravel, you should know its weight on leaving a depot; for palleted cargo, you should know the weight of each pallet.

EU and national rules govern the maximum weights of different kinds of truck, and you are responsible for ensuring that your truck is in compliance.

Údarás Um Shábháilteacht Ar Bhóithre
Road Safety Authority

Your daily walk-around check

Your daily walk-around check is an essential first step in an effective preventative maintenance system. You should use it to:

- Identify obvious vehicle defects so they can be fixed; and
- Make sure that the vehicle is in a roadworthy condition before you drive it on the road.

Get into the habit of carrying out the daily walk-around check on the truck before you start your first journey of the day. Even if you are not the first driver to drive the truck in a day, you should still carry out the walk-around to satisfy yourself as to the roadworthiness and safety of the truck. A basic check will take you no more than a few minutes, and should include the whole vehicle, including the trailer, where there is one. The following tables present a comprehensive checklist that you can use for your daily walk-around.

See also

The RSA website has detailed guidelines on daily walk-around checks.

Enter walk-around in the Search box on the RSA website's home page (www.rsa.ie)

External checks on all trucks

These are checks that you can make by walking around the truck (and the trailer, if there is one).

Tax, insurance, haulage licence discs	Check that the tax and insurance discs are present, valid and within date. Where necessary, also make sure the haulage licence is valid and within date.
Tyres	Check the tyre pressure and tread depth – the legal minimum tyre tread depth is 1.6mm. Check for any visible defects in the tyres – such as cuts, cracks or bulges.
Wheels	Check that no wheel nuts are missing and that all wheel nuts are secure and correctly fitted. If wheel nut pointers are fitted, they enable you to see at a glance if any of the nuts have loosened. Check for any cracks or damage on wheels.
Lights and reflectors	Check that all required lights are fitted, clean and working correctly. It will be quicker if you have a colleague help you with this or you could have a fixed mirror in your yard so that lights can be checked from the cab. Check that all the required reflective markings are fitted, and that they are clearly visible and not faded.
Exhaust	Check for any signs of the exhaust being loose or excessively noisy.
Suspension	Check that the air suspension is set at the correct drive height and make sure that springs are not damaged or broken.
Truck body and fittings	Check that: • All cab and trailer doors are secure and properly closed; • All body panels are secure; • Bodywork is undamaged and has no sharp edges; • All straps, chains, curtains and restraining devices are securely fastened; and • Items such as tail lifts and cranes are securely stowed.
Number plates and marker plates	Check that the number plates are fitted in the correct position and that they are clean and clearly legible. Where a trailer is attached, it must display the truck's number plates at the rear, and it must also display its own registration or marker plate on the near-side chassis rail.

Fluids	Check that all fluid levels are between minimum and maximum levels – in some trucks, fluid levels are indicated on in-cab gauges. Check that there are no leaks or spills of oil or fuel around the truck.
Air tanks	Make sure that the air tanks are free of moisture, and drain them if necessary (if this is not done automatically).
Steps / catwalks	Make sure that all steps and catwalks are secure.
Air and electrical suzies and connectors	Check that all required service leads and connectors (including ABS and EBS cables if applicable) are correctly in place and in good condition. There should be no leaks from the air lines or evidence of stretching, chafing or general damage or wear.
Coupling – fifth wheel or drawbar	Check that the trailer is correctly coupled to the truck, either: - The trailer is correctly located on the fifth wheel; or - The trailer is securely coupled with a drawbar.

In-cab checks

Make the following checks every time you sit into the cab of a truck.

Mirrors	Check that all rear-view and close-proximity mirrors and kerb mirrors are secure and aligned correctly.
Windows	Check the windows for cracks or other damage or anything that could obscure your vision while driving.
Driver's seat / seat belt / head restraint	Check that the driver's seat is adjusted so that you can reach all of the controls. Make sure the seatbelt is working correctly and that the head restraint is correctly adjusted.
Horn	Check that the horn works.
Speed limiter	Where applicable, check that a speed limiter plaque is fitted and that it is showing the same tyre size as on the vehicle drive axle.
Windscreen washer and wipers	Check that the wipers work correctly and the blades are not worn. Check that the windscreen washer works and the jets are aimed correctly. If necessary, top up the windscreen washer fluid reservoir.
The tachograph	Make sure that the hours and calibration are correct. - For digital tachographs, make sure that the unit is operating and there is paper loaded in the printer. - For analogue tachographs, insert a new chart into the unit and make sure it is operating correctly.

ABS and EBS in-cab warning lights	Check that the ABS or EBS lights display and follow their correct sequence.
Instruments, gauges, warning devices	Check that no instrument warning lights or indicators remain on after start-up.
Air leaks and pressure drops	Check for any indications of a drop in brake air pressure, for example: ⭕ The sound of an air leak; ⭕ Air warning lights or buzzer; and ⭕ The air pressure gauge showing insufficient pressure.

Further checks before you leave the depot

There are some further checks you should make with the engine started, before you leave the depot and take the truck onto the public road.

Brakes	Check the service brake on both tractor and trailer. Check there are no air leaks when you press the brake. Check that the brake pedal is free from damage and there is adequate anti-slip provision on the pedal.
Steering	Check that the steering does not have too much play and operates freely when the power assistance is in operation.
Load security and weight distribution	Check that all loads are adequately secured and unlikely to move during the journey. Make sure that the truck is not overloaded (either overall or on any individual axle). Check that the load is not too wide, too high or too long. See **Minding your load** (on page 27) for more information on minding and securing your load.

Vehicle servicing

You are responsible for ensuring that the truck you take on the road is in a roadworthy condition and that it has been maintained and serviced correctly in line with the manufacturer's guidelines.

You should also confirm that the truck has a valid and up-to-date Certificate of Roadworthiness – see page 64 for more information on this.

Údarás Um Shábháilteacht Ar Bhóithre
Road Safety Authority

Driver Walk-Around Check Sheet

You must make sure that the vehicle you are driving is roadworthy and is not likely to cause danger to anyone.

Driver's Name:_____ Signature_____
Date:_____ Vehicle Reg:_____ Mileage:_____

Check Items	Tick box if defect found
In-Cab Checks	
1. Good visibility through all cab windows and mirrors. Mirrors adjusted properly.	
2. Driving controls, seat, and safety belts.	
3. Windscreen washer and wipers.	
4. Horn.	
5. Tachograph correct hours and calibration and speed limiter plaque displayed.	
6. ABS/EBS in-cab warning lights.	
7. All instruments, gauges, & warning devices.	
8. Check for air leaks and pressure drop.	
External Vehicle Checks	
9. Check tax and insurance discs are present and valid.	
10. Wheels for condition and security. Tyres for damage, correct inflation, and tread depth.	
11. All lights and reflectors.	
12. Exhaust.	
13. Air & electrical suzies and connectors.	
14. Fifth wheel and locking devices, steps, catwalk, or drawbar coupling.	
15. Vehicle body/wings/guards, side and rear / curtains and straps/doors/tail lift.	
16. Landing legs and handle.	
17. Trailer park brake (operation).	
18. Air suspension correctly set.	
19. Number plates and marker plates.	
20. Check engine oil, water, windscreen washer reservoir, and fuel – for levels and leaks.	
Prior to Leaving Depot	
21. Steering and brake operation.	
22. Load security and weight distribution.	
On-the-Road	
23. Tachograph, speedometer, and speed limiter.	
24. ABS/EBS warning lights off.	

Example of the type of walk-around check sheet that is common in the road transport industry.

Údarás Um Shábháilteacht Ar Bhóithre
Road Safety Authority

On-the-road checks

Once you are on the road, there are some ongoing checks you should make in the first few kilometres.

Tachograph	Check that the tachograph continues to operate correctly.
Speedometer / speed limiter	Check that the speedometer is working correctly and you can see it from the driving position.
ABS and EBS warning lights	Check that the ABS or EBS lights do not remain on after their check sequence is complete, as this may indicate a fault with the system. Check the vehicle manual for guidance before you set off on your journey.

My commitment: 2

I will not take a truck on the road without first carrying out a walk-around check to identify any visible defects and to make sure that the truck is in a roadworthy condition.

Signed (Learner)

Minding your load

Trucks are used to carry all kinds of goods and materials, and as a truck driver you are responsible for making sure that the load you carry is safely restrained and not likely to constitute a hazard on the road. You must be satisfied that the truck you are driving is suitable for transporting the load – this could be an issue for perishable goods, live animals, or goods that need to be protected from the weather. You should also check that your load is secure from theft.

The checks you make before you set out on a journey will depend on the particular type of truck you have and the goods you are carrying, but you should check some or all of the following:

- All external ropes, straps and chains are securely fastened, and not likely to flap in the wind or cause a hazard to other road users;
- Doors, shutters and tailgates are locked, and locking handles are secured (where present);
- All hatches are correctly closed (for example, on liquid tankers); and
- The load is balanced as much as possible so that each axle is taking roughly the same weight and also that each wheel is taking the same weight. This will help the stability of the truck on the road.

See also

The European Commission's *European Best Practice Guidelines on Cargo Securing for Road Transport* gives detailed guidance about securing cargo. This is available online at:

http://ec.europa.eu/transport/road_safety/vehicles/doc/cargo_securing_guidelines_en.pdf

More than a truck driver

Different kinds of trucks come with different kinds of extra equipment such as tail lifts and cranes that the driver needs to be able to operate competently. There is also a great variety of special purpose trucks with built-in functionality – these include cement lorries, refrigerated trucks, skip trucks, tipper trucks, vehicle transporters and fuel tankers, to name but a few.

Most trucking and transport companies train their drivers in how to use devices such as specialist loading equipment. As the driver, however, you take responsibility for the carriage of the goods in the truck, and for that reason, you need to be competent in the use of any loading or unloading equipment.

Route planning

As a professional truck driver, your job will involve transporting goods safely and efficiently from one location to another. The better you plan your routes, the less stressful your journey will be and you can also achieve greater fuel efficiency.

The consequences of not planning journeys adequately can be much more serious for truck drivers than for drivers of smaller vehicles – for example, you do not want to find yourself having to reverse out of a narrow street that you turned into in error or because you did not have clear route directions.

Issues that you need to consider in route planning include:

- Time of day – try to avoid the morning and evening rush hours in locations that you know become congested;
- Clearway areas, in which you are not permitted to stop or park at certain times;
- Low railway bridges;
- Bridges with weight restrictions;
- Narrow roads and streets that might not be suitable for large vehicles;
- Pedestrianised streets; and
- Streets or districts that are prohibited to large vehicles.

Route planning is particularly important if your journey involves multiple deliveries, and you will need to ensure that your cargo is loaded in an efficient manner for delivery – typically, 'last on: first off'.

Route planning tools

Among the tools that you can use to help with route planning are:

- Road maps, such as those published by the Ordnance Survey;
- Satellite navigation systems;
- Online resources for route planning; and
- Radio traffic bulletins.

3. Gaining experience on the road

In this chapter

Learning to drive a truck involves practising the various skills that you need to learn, and the best way to do that is with a qualified ADI. This chapter gives an outline of the skills that you need to focus on.

It begins with learning how to start the truck, move off and stop, and how to move through the low gears. It moves on to your first on-the-road practice with your ADI and how you 'read' the road and know how to position the truck on the road. Keeping up with traffic, managing your speed, and dealing with all kinds of junctions and roundabouts are all important skills to learn, and you will only learn these by practice. You also need to practise manoeuvres such as reversing, parking and starting on hills.

While you are practising, you will draw on all your experience as a car driver, but you will need to improve your observational skills to recognise early the potential hazards and challenges that you face. Dealing with the size of the truck and the absence of a central mirror are among the greatest challenges you face.

Once you have passed your truck driving test and gained your full licence, you can drive on motorways – this chapter also describes some of the challenges you will face in motorway driving.

Starting and stopping the truck: the first time

Your ADI will make sure that your first experience of starting a truck is in a safe environment – for example, an empty car park, disused road, or similar location.

Starting the engine

Before you turn the key in the ignition, check that the parking brake is **on** and that the gear lever is in NEUTRAL.

For most trucks, you turn the key clockwise and allow it to spring back when the engine starts running. This should take no more than a second or so.

If your truck has a different starting mechanism (such as a start button) and you are not sure how to use it, ask your ADI to show you how it works.

You need to get to know the sound of the engine. So, with the gear lever still in NEUTRAL, gently press the accelerator once or twice so you can hear the change in the engine sound.

Moving off and stopping

Moving off and stopping for the first time is not easy, and the only way you'll learn it is to do it. The principles of moving off and stopping are similar to those for a car, but it can take a while to get used to the great difference in the truck's size and power.

Moving off from the kerb

As you practise starting and moving off, get into the habit of checking your mirror, signalling and checking your blind spots (including cyclops mirror) before you actually move off. This is the **Mirror–Signal–Mirror (blind spots)–Manoeuvre** routine.

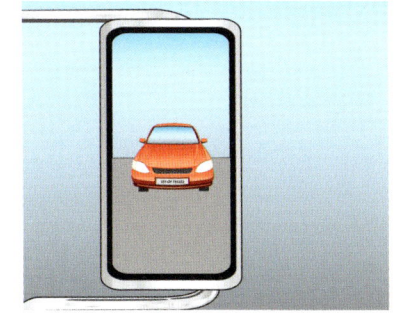

1. Mirror
Look in your mirrors (left and right) to check that it is safe to move out. Use the cyclops mirror also – see the Note on page 32.

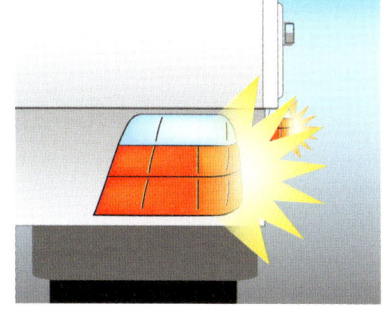

2. Signal
Signal your intention to move by turning on an indicator.

3. Mirror and check blind spots
Check your mirrors again (left and right) and check your blind spots.

Be particularly aware of other vehicles, pedestrians and cyclists before you move off.

4. Manoeuvre
Move off smoothly in the correct gear and with good control of the clutch, accelerator and brakes.

From 1 October 2012, all HGVs (Heavy Goods Vehicles) with a DGVW (Design Gross Vehicle Weight) exceeding 7,500kg, regardless of age, must be fitted with a Class VI mirror, or 'cyclops' mirror to provide a clear view of the blind spot at the front of the vehicle.

If you have not already fitted a cyclops mirror, it's time to do so. The fitting and correct adjustment of this mirror will be checked at your vehicle's annual roadworthiness test from 1 October 2012.

Steering the truck

As you are practising moving off and driving short distances, get used to the feel of the steering wheel and how the truck responds to the steering adjustments you make. Don't worry if you understeer or oversteer at the beginning. You'll soon be able to make very precise adjustments in the steering. Practise steering the truck to very precise points.

Hold the steering wheel with both hands, firmly but not too tightly. The position of your hands on the wheel should be comfortable and give you most control.

Most trucks have power-assisted steering and don't require much physical effort.

Changing gears

In the early stages of learning to drive a truck, you need to master smooth and efficient use of the gears. The range of gears available depends on the truck you are practising on, and there are wide variations in the number and use of gears. Your ADI will advise you about the gears on the particular truck you are driving.

My commitment: 3

I am able to start the truck, drive a few metres and stop the truck in a safe location.

I am able to drive the truck in a safe location and can change gears competently.

Signed (Learner)

Braking

The amount of downward pressure you put on the brake determines how quickly the truck will slow down and stop.

In the normal course of driving, you should aim to brake early and progressively. In other words, don't wait until just before you need to stop to put your foot on the brake – slow down in advance by pressing gently on the brake, and then pressing more firmly to come to a complete stop. This will give you and your cargo a smoother ride, it is easier on the truck, and will save you fuel.

When you are braking you need to take into account that a fully loaded vehicle takes a longer distance to come to a complete stop than an empty one.

Trucks with automatic or semi-automatic transmission

Some modern trucks use automatic or semi-automatic transmission and there is wide variation in how the transmission works – depending on the make and model of the truck. For example, some trucks have semi-automatic gearboxes that give you full control over what gear the truck is in, but have no clutch pedal. In other trucks you might find a sophisticated computer-controlled gearbox that selects the appropriate gear based on road and driving conditions.

If you are unsure about how the transmission works in the truck you are practising in, ask your ADI to show you. For all trucks with automatic or semi-automatic gearboxes, you must be able to hold the truck stationary with the footbrake before you move off.

Each time you sit at the wheel of an unfamiliar truck, take the time to study the transmission system, and don't take the truck on the road until you are sure you know how it works.

Your first time on the road

Your first time driving a truck on the public road should be in light traffic. While you are driving, your ADI will point out any potential hazards and will give you clear instructions. You need to:

- Drive at a safe and appropriate speed;
- Keep an eye on your mirrors;
- Look out for any potential hazards; and
- Keep a safe distance from the vehicle in front of you and from vehicles parked on the side of the road.

Practice tip

Even if you are one of the small number of people who choose to learn independently, you are recommended to book a lesson with an approved driving instructor (ADI) for your first experience of driving a truck on a public road. Trucks provided by ADIs for learner training have dual controls, and the instructors themselves have the know-how and the experience to make your first trip a safe learning experience.

Údarás Um Shábháilteacht Ar Bhóithre
Road Safety Authority

Combining knowledge and practice

The first time you drive a truck on the public road you will probably still be getting used to the size and weight of the truck, to its controls, and to the very different way it handles (compared to a car). There are three main areas to concentrate on:

1.	Controlling the truck and its position on the road, and leaving enough space between the truck and parked vehicles and vulnerable road users such as pedestrians and cyclists..
2.	Reading the road signs and understanding how they apply to you as a truck driver (and obeying mandatory signs).
3.	Observing and anticipating what other road users are doing; and giving them advance warning of what you are going to do.

On the public road

While you are driving on the public road, you need to:

- Maintain a speed that is appropriate to the road conditions;
- Scan the road ahead and to the sides at all times, and also keep an eye in your mirrors to check what's coming behind you; and
- Check your mirrors and signal before you make manoeuvres such as changing lane or turning at a junction.

My commitment: 4
I am able to drive the truck on the public road in a quiet location in very light traffic.
Signed (Learner)

Planning practice journeys

With the help of your ADI, you need to gradually take on more challenging journeys. Plan a number of practice journeys over the course of a number of weeks. Your practice journeys should include all of the following:

- Turning onto and off main roads
- Negotiating roundabouts
- Reversing
- Overtaking a slow-moving vehicle
- Changing lanes
- Starting on a hill (uphill and downhill)
- Stopping and moving off at traffic lights

Every journey you make can give you valuable experience and present new challenges. As you become more competent and confident, your practice journeys will take place in heavier traffic, on roads with sharper curves, and in more difficult driving conditions. While you are practising, your ADI will give you advice about potential hazards and handling traffic.

Reading the road

As you drive along any road you are receiving information all the time, and you need to be able to take in this information and respond appropriately.

Scan the road as you drive, and get into the habit of observing all of the information that road markings and road signs give you. Remember to obey the *Rules of the Road* and to follow all traffic controls at all times. Be particularly alert for any hazards that arise as you drive, and listen to any advice that your ADI gives you.

The size of the truck (compared to a car) means that some road features can represent hazards for a truck, even if they would not for a car.

For example, depending on the road camber, the top of the truck might be leaning to the left and in danger of striking lamp posts or overhanging bushes.

Processing information

As a truck driver, you should continually scan the environment and take into account traffic controls, road markings, regulatory warnings and directional signs.

My commitment: 5
I am able to 'read the road' – to take in the information I need from road markings, regulatory and warning signs, traffic lights, and direction signs.
Signed (Learner)

Every time you take a truck onto the road, your first concern is with safety – your own safety and that of all other road users.

Knowing your position on the road

Knowing your position on the road and being able to steer accurately and precisely are essential skills to acquire. In the early stages of practice, learner truck drivers often have difficulty getting used to the size of the truck and visualising its position on the road. You need to know or visualise where the front and back of the truck are in relation to other road users and road 'furniture' (such as bollards), and where the sides of the truck are in relation to the kerb, parked cars and lane markings.

Where lanes are marked	Where lanes are not marked
Position the truck centrally between the lane markers. If you need to change lanes, follow the **Mirror** – **Signal** – **Mirror (blind spots)** – **Manoeuvre** routine. If you are going to turn off to the left or right, plan ahead so that you are in the correct lane when you arrive at the junction – and keep in mind that you need to plan further ahead than you would in a car.	Keep to the left as you drive – but not too close to the verge or to parked vehicles or the pavement (in urban areas).

 Observing the position of cars and other vehicles ahead and behind you will give you a sense of where you should be on the road.

Keep your distance

Don't drive too close to the vehicle in front of you. The faster the traffic is moving, the greater the distance you should allow.

The distance it will take you to stop in an emergency depends on many things, including how alert you are, the type and condition of the road surface, and how good your brakes and tyres are.

The *Rules of the Road* sets out the stopping distances for cars at different speeds in different road conditions. For trucks, however, stopping distances are usually much greater, and can be up to twice or three times that for cars in the same road and weather conditions.

Never 'tailgate' the vehicle in front of you. If that vehicle brakes suddenly, you may be unable to avoid colliding with it. You should leave a greater distance to the front if there is a vehicle very close behind trying to overtake you – this will make it easier for the vehicle behind you to overtake you and then return to the left-hand lane. It will also reduce the risks associated with the overtaking driver's behaviour.

My commitment: 6
I know how to position my truck on the road: I maintain a safe distance between my truck and the vehicle ahead; I understand how lanes work and can position my truck in the appropriate position at all times while driving.
Signed (Learner)

Dealing with junctions

In the course of your driving practice, you should try to meet as many different kinds of junction as possible. The manoeuvres you perform should include making left and right turns, crossing junctions, using filter lanes, turning at box junctions, entering and exiting roundabouts, and so on.

The *Rules of the Road* gives comprehensive guidance on how you should approach and drive at junctions.

Driving on a major road

When you are driving on a major road, you generally have priority over traffic emerging from minor roads. Advance signs of junctions ahead are for your information – they're not telling you to do anything, except to exercise caution and to be aware that cars and other traffic may be waiting to join the main road or to turn off onto the minor road.

Don't overtake in advance of a junction. A driver turning left from a side road to the right might not have checked traffic coming from his or her left.

Turning at a junction

Turning at a junction in a truck is much more difficult than in a car, and there are some potential hazards that you need to look out for.

A truck needs space in order to make a turn, and making turns correctly requires you to manage the road space that is available to you to best effect. Where possible, you should always take the space you need from the road you are leaving, and not from the road you are entering – see Taking space at junctions on page 40.

As you approach a junction at which you want to turn, check your mirrors, signal in advance, and slow down smoothly.

The course that you take when turning (left or right) depends on the width, length and overhang of the truck and on the road space available. You will sometimes need to adjust your position to give yourself a better turning angle and to avoid touching the kerb and any railings or bollards.

If you are emerging from a minor road, your sight lines might not be very good, so look both ways – there could be bends or dips in the roadway or overhanging bushes in rural areas. In urban areas, watch out for parked cars or goods vehicles and for buses setting down or taking on passengers. Also, a slow-moving bus or truck could obscure a car that is about to overtake it.

Tail swing

Be aware of the possibility of 'tail swing' when you are turning, left or right. This is the way the rear of the truck swings or pivots in the opposite direction to that in which you are turning. This is more likely on trucks with a long overhang behind the rear axle.

Front overhang

In certain situations (particularly when you are turning at a sharp angle) the front of the trailer swings in a much wider arc than the cab, and you need to be careful that the front corner of the trailer does not collide with anything – for example, road signs, traffic signals, lamp posts, walls or buildings.

- When you are turning right, you need to check the left front side of the trailer; and
- When you are turning left, you need to check the right front side of the trailer.

You also need to be particularly careful turning when the front of the trailer overhangs the cab – for example, in car transporters.

For all turns

For all turns, left and right, you need to:

- Make sure there is nothing blocking your entry to the road you are turning into – the space available must be able to accommodate the full length of your truck;
- Check your mirrors for following traffic before you make the turn – in particular, for cyclists or for any vehicles that could be trying to overtake you;
- Wait until there is a safe gap in oncoming traffic before making the turn;
- Give way to any pedestrians already crossing the road you are entering; and
- Allow more time to complete the turn than you would in a car.

For left turns

When you are turning left at a junction, steer a course that is wide enough to ensure that you do not touch the kerb with your left-side rear wheels. Make sure there are no pedestrians, cyclists or other road users on your inside. Do not cut across cyclists who are going straight ahead.

For right turns

When you are turning right at a junction, move closer to the left centre of the road or use the turning lane where this is provided.

At T-junctions

Before turning at a T-junction, look left and right to ensure that it is safe to make the turn.

Údarás Um Shábháilteacht Ar Bhóithre
Road Safety Authority

Taking space at junctions

Taking the space from the road you are leaving helps to avoid unforeseen problems in the road you are entering.

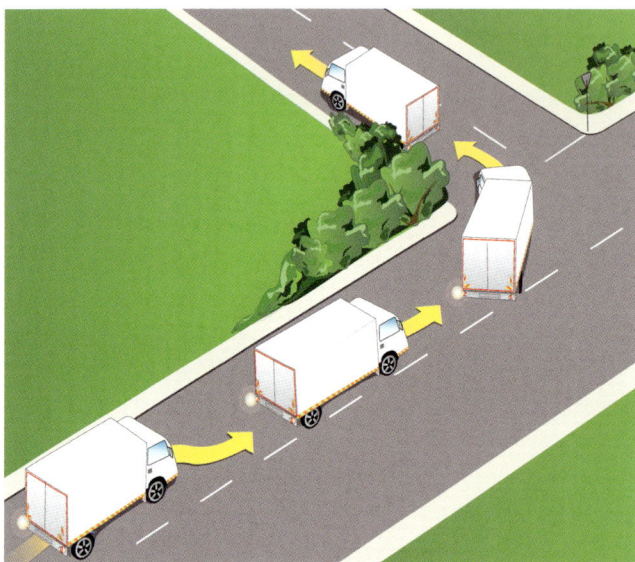

Turning left from a major to a minor road

In this case, the truck turning left moves to the left centre of the road it is leaving – to avoid touching the pavement on the corner.

Turning left from a minor to a major road

In this case the truck moves to the left centre of the minor road in order to get a safer angle at which to enter the main road.

Turning right from a major to a minor road

In this case, the truck uses the turning lane and progresses far enough through the junction to ensure that it does not cut across any traffic waiting to exit the minor road.

 **Note** The speed appropriate to a minor road you are joining might be considerably less than the speed you've been driving at on the major road.

Slip roads

Slip roads are designed to make it easy to join and leave major roads, including motorways and dual carriageways.

Joining a major road	Signal your intention to join the main road and give way to traffic already on it. Your speed should be close to that of traffic already on the main road. Where there are two slip lanes, you should ideally use the left-hand lane.
Leaving a major road	Move into the correct lane well in advance of the slip road and signal your intention to leave the main road.

Junctions with traffic lights

Some junctions with traffic lights are simple; others are complex. Before you proceed through a green light, be sure that it applies to you. For example, at complex junctions, a green arrow light might apply to traffic going straight on, but not to traffic turning left or right.

If a traffic light has been green for quite a while as you approach it, be prepared to stop when it turns amber.

Yellow box junctions

You must not enter a yellow box junction unless you can clear it without stopping. An exception is when you want to turn right. In this case, you may enter the yellow box junction while waiting for a gap in traffic coming from the opposite direction. However, don't enter the box if to do so would block other traffic that has the right of way.

Yellow box junctions can also be found at railway level crossings and tramway crossings. Never enter these yellow box junctions unless you can leave them without stopping.

Roundabouts

The advantage of roundabouts over other types of junction is that traffic flows more smoothly. For the learner truck driver, however, roundabouts present particular challenges. Keep the following points in mind:

- Your choice of lane might be restricted by the size of the truck – for example, on a tight roundabout, it might not be possible to stay within the road markings;
- You need to check the direction signs and road markings more carefully than usual – your exit might not be 'obvious';
- It can be difficult to see across the roundabout to where you want to go – this is particularly the case with large roundabouts with many exits;
- You might need to cross lanes (from right to left) to get to the exit you want – while at the same time other drivers may be trying to cross in the opposite direction (from left to right);
- As with other busy junctions, there might be pedestrians crossing;
- You might not have to stop as you approach a roundabout, but you must yield to traffic already on the roundabout and to traffic coming from the right; and
- You might need to drive over a mini-roundabout – depending on the size of your truck.

Exiting to the left	If your exit is to the left (9 o'clock), approach the roundabout in the left-hand lane (if there is one) and signal 'left'.
Exiting straight ahead	If your exit is straight ahead (12 o'clock), approach the roundabout in the left-hand lane (if there is one and unless the road markings indicate otherwise) and signal 'left' after you have cleared the exit before the one you want.
Exiting to the right	If your exit is to the right (after 12 o'clock), approach the roundabout in the right-hand lane (if there is one), and signal 'right'. Make sure you follow the **Mirror – Signal – Mirror (blind spots) – Manoeuvre** routine. Signal to exit (left) after you have cleared the exit before the one you want.

Depending on the road space available, you may need to straddle two lanes to complete these manoeuvres safely – particularly on smaller roundabouts.

Road Safety Authority

Reading the direction signs at roundabouts

Roundabouts are usually well sign-posted – both with an advance sign and signs at each exit. The advance sign shows the layout of the roundabout showing where each exit leads to. You should note which of the exits is the one you want – first, second, third and so on.

Be alert to other drivers' signals when you are on a roundabout. Be prepared that other drivers might cross in front of you when changing lanes to get to an exit.

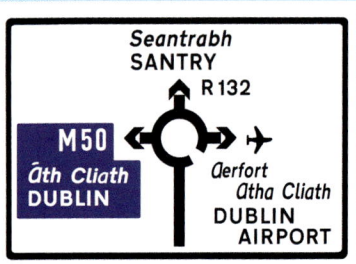

In this example, a driver intending to drive to Santry would take the second exit.

At the roundabout, each exit is clearly marked.

See also

Using roundabouts

For more information on roundabouts, see the video 'Using roundabouts' on the RSA website. To locate the video, type **roundabouts** in the Search box on the home page and then click on **Search**.

My commitment: 7

I can safely negotiate all types of road junction – including left and right turns (from major to minor and from minor to major roads), slip roads, junctions with traffic lights, and roundabouts.

Signed (Learner)

Controlling your speed

Excessive speed is a contributory factor in many collisions. The *Rules of the Road* sets out the maximum speed at which you may travel on different types of road.

The maximum speed limit for trucks is 80km/h. Even if you are travelling on a national primary road or a motorway, you must obey this limit.

There are also local variations indicated by signs posted along the roadside. These can be temporary (for example, where there are road works), or permanent (at locations where the local authority has imposed a speed limit for various safety reasons).

Driving at an even, moderate speed

On the open road, drive at an even speed – don't speed up and slow down for no reason, and avoid having to brake suddenly in the normal course of driving.

Moderate your speed in bad weather conditions, or if there are a lot of pedestrians around, or if the road is very narrow.

Adjust your speed evenly and smoothly, both when you are accelerating and when you are slowing down – this is safer and uses less fuel.

Check your speedometer regularly. You might be travelling faster than you think – especially if you are driving in a town or suburb immediately after you have been driving on a higher speed road (such as a dual carriageway).

Slowing down at bends

Dangerous bends and corners are generally indicated by warning signs on the side of the road. These indicate the direction and sharpness of the turn.

As you approach a bend, you need to judge your own speed and decide whether or not you need to slow down. Where the road marking SLOW is shown in advance of the bend, reduce your speed.

If necessary, change down gears as you approach a sharp bend, and then gently accelerate through and out of the bend.

Signalling your intentions

Communicating and cooperating with other road users is very important for road safety. You need to let other road users know what you are about to do and you need to correctly interpret signals that other drivers give you. The most important signals you can use are your indicators but, in different circumstances, you can also use your horn or hand signals. Your brake lights and reversing lights also help to let other road users know what you are doing.

When to use your indicators

Use your indicator to signal when you intend to change direction, in particular when you want to:

- Turn (left or right) onto another road;
- Turn off at a roundabout exit;
- Change lanes;
- Overtake a slower-moving vehicle;
- Move around an obstruction – for example, a bus that has pulled in at a bus stop; or
- Pull into or out of a parking space.

Turn the indicator on early to let other road users know what you are going to do, but not so early that you are likely to cause confusion.

Make the turn when it is safe to do so – just turning on the indicator does not give you the automatic right to turn. For example, when turning right off a main road, you must yield to traffic coming against you, and you must always yield to pedestrians already crossing the road. There may be situations where you have to be especially careful about when to give the signal – for example, if there are two left turns, one very close after the other.

Make sure your indicator is turned off after you complete the manoeuvre.

Brake lights

Every time you put your foot on the brake, your brake lights come on and this gives a signal to the vehicles behind you that you are slowing down.

Note: If your truck is pulling a trailer, it is essential to check that all the service leads (suzies) are properly connected *before* you leave the depot or yard – including air lines for the brakes and electric lines for the brake lights.

Using your horn

Your truck's horn is a very important safety device. You can use the horn to warn other road users if you think they might not have seen you. Only use a horn to warn other road users of oncoming danger, or to make them aware of your presence when reasonably necessary for safety reasons.

Using the horn does not give you the right of way.

My commitment: 8
I know when to signal my intentions to other road users – including when to use direction indicators and the horn.
Signed (Learner)

Interpreting other road users' intentions

A safe and responsible truck driver is able to interpret other road users' signals. Sometimes you will have to second-guess what other people are going to do. Flashing direction indicators are the easiest to interpret, but you will learn to interpret a wide range of signals, intended and unintended, that other road users give. The use of signals, however, does not give a right of way.

Other drivers signal their intentions clearly when they turn on their indicators or apply their brakes. But they also signal their intentions in more subtle ways – for example, by changing speed, by changing lane or changing direction, by pulling in to the side of the road, and so on. Not every driver will signal their intentions clearly.

You need to develop:

- **Skills of observation** … so that you notice subtle changes in other road users' behaviour; and
- **Skills of interpretation** … so that you can correctly interpret what these changes in behaviour mean.

Don't always trust other road users to do the right thing or to do what they say they're going to do – being 'in the right' might not be much consolation if you have a collision. One common error that some motorists make is not turning off the indicator after a turn.

Observation skills (anticipation and reaction)

Developing your skills of observation is a key part of becoming a safe and competent truck driver. You need to know what's going on around you at all times. Always scan the road ahead (near and far) to anticipate situations before they become dangerous. And the faster you are travelling, the further ahead you will need to look.

Using your mirrors

Your truck's mirrors help you see what's coming behind. Scan your mirrors regularly so you know what's going on, and always check in your mirrors before any manoeuvre such as changing lanes or turning into a different road.

Remember to check your blind spots before certain manoeuvres – for example, when you are pulling out into traffic from a parking place, or changing lanes or direction.

Because bicycles and motorcycles have such a narrow profile, cyclists can easily become 'hidden' in a blind spot. Be particularly careful to check your blind spot before you open your truck door. Also, be particularly careful turning left – check that there is no other road user on your inside.

Be aware that your mirrors might be slightly convex to give you a wider field of view. This, however, will make things you see in them seem further away than they actually are.

My commitment: 9
I can interpret other road users' intentions – from the signals they give and also from subtle changes in their behaviour.
Signed (Learner)

Reversing

Being able to reverse the truck accurately is an important skill, and one you should begin to practise in a safe, traffic-free location.

The main difference between reversing a truck and reversing a car is that in a truck you have to rely on your side mirrors, and depending on the angle you are turning at, you might be able to see behind on one side only. Also the back end of the truck is much further away from you, and it can take a while for a learner truck driver to judge that distance when reversing.

Practise reversing with the help of your ADI – first in a straight line, and then to the left and right, and into precise locations.

As with a car, the steering in a truck is usually controlled by the front wheels, so when you are reversing the effect of turning the steering wheel is not quite as immediate as when you are going in a forward direction. Being good at reversing is an essential skill for a truck driver, as you will need to be able to reverse when parking, pulling into a loading bay and getting out of awkward locations.

Before you begin a truck reversing manoeuvre, you must satisfy yourself that there are no obstacles or hazards. If necessary, walk around the truck in advance. Drive slowly while you are reversing to ensure that you remain in control at all times. You should also check all around periodically.

Using a helper to guide you when reversing

There will be times when you will need someone outside the truck to guide you as you reverse – for example, into a loading bay. And there will be times when you might be able to help a fellow truck driver.

The helper should wear a hi-vis vest, and should give strong clear signals. You should be able to see the helper in the mirror at all times – if you can't, stop.

My commitment: 10
I have practised reversing the truck, including straight, left and right reversing.
I will always exercise great caution when reversing, and will reverse only when I am sure that there are no obstacles or hazards behind the truck.
Signed (Learner)

Parking

As a truck driver, you need to be able to park in order to make deliveries and access loading bays and depots. Learning to park a truck means mastering control of the truck in confined spaces at low speed, in both forward and reverse gears.

Before you begin any parking manoeuvre, you need to be sure that the truck will fit in the space you want to reverse into. Locations where trucks make deliveries or load up usually have spaces that are large enough to accommodate a truck. In other locations, you may have to take up two or more standard car parking spaces.

When parking at the side of the road, make sure that your truck is parked legally and that it will not cause an obstruction or a hazard to other road users.

If you have to reverse to park (or to leave a parking space), make sure that it is safe to do so and if necessary ask someone to guide you.

My commitment: 11
I am able to manoeuvre the truck very precisely at low speeds in forward and reverse gears.
I have practised parking the truck in a variety of locations.
Signed (Learner)

Coupling and uncoupling a trailer

Drivers of articulated trucks need to be able to couple and uncouple a trailer to and from the tractor unit. The first time you carry out these procedures, you should be accompanied by a competent and experienced driver or ADI who can lead you through the procedures safely and correctly.

For both coupling and uncoupling, the exact steps to follow will depend on the individual tractor and trailer. The steps outlined below are generic steps that apply in most cases.

 Before you couple a trailer to a tractor unit, you should check that the trailer has a valid Certificate of Roadworthiness, and that it has a Vehicle Weights and Dimensions Plate.

Coupling a trailer

Before you begin to couple your tractor unit to a trailer, there are a number of safety checks that you need to make:

- Check that the doors of the trailer are securely closed, and that it is not still being loaded;
- Advise any person nearby that you are about to couple the trailer;
- Check that the height of the trailer matches that of the tractor so that the fifth wheel will fit beneath the trailer – you might need to adjust the air suspension in the cab if the tractor is too high or too low;
- Make sure that you are on level ground, that the trailer brake is applied and wheel chocks are in place; and
- Make sure that the tractor and trailer are lined up correctly and not at an angle to each other.

Step	Description
1	Reverse the tractor unit slowly up to the front of the trailer until the kingpin locking mechanism clicks into place on the fifth wheel of the tractor – you should hear the 'click' when this happens.
2	Ensure that the locking mechanism is secure by selecting a low gear and attempting to drive forward. If the trailer is securely coupled, you should feel the resistance.
3	Apply the parking brake and turn off the engine before leaving the tractor unit. Inspect the coupling visually to check that the fifth wheel has correctly engaged with the kingpin of the trailer. Connect the dog clip (where fitted) to secure the kingpin release handle.
4	Connect the air and electric lines (suzies), and turn on taps (where fitted). To access the suzies, you may have to open or fold back an access panel – close this securely when you have finished.
5	Use the winding handle to raise the landing gear on the trailer as far up as it will go. Stow the handle securely when you have finished. Remove the wheel chocks and release the trailer brake.
6	Get back in the cab, and start the engine. Check that all gauges register correct pressures in the air tanks and that no warning lights or buzzers come on.
7	Check that all the lights are working and that there are no air line leaks – if possible, ask someone standing outside the truck to help you with this.
8	Secure the correct number plate to the back of the trailer, and make sure that the lights and reflectors are clean. Carry out a full walk-around check on the tractor and trailer before you begin any journey – see page 22.

Uncoupling a trailer

Before you uncouple a trailer, make sure that you are on firm, level ground. If you are uncoupling at a loading bay, you will need to secure the rear doors open before you begin.

Step	Description
1	Apply the brakes on the tractor unit and switch off the engine.
2	Put wheel chocks in place on the trailer wheels and apply the trailer brakes.
3	Use the winding handle to lower the landing gear on the trailer. Stow the handle securely when you have finished.
4	Disconnect the air and electric lines (suzies), and turn off taps (where fitted). Stow the lines safely. To access the suzies, you may have to open or fold back an access panel – close this securely when you have finished.
5	Remove the dog clip (where fitted) securing the kingpin release handle.
6	Release the fifth wheel coupling locking bar (where fitted).
7	Drive the tractor unit forward slowly, checking the trailer either directly or in the mirrors.
8	Remove the number plate from the back of the trailer.

Overtaking

You should always be extremely careful when overtaking a slower-moving vehicle and should always ask yourself these questions:

Is it necessary?	If you are going to turn off the road a few hundred metres further on, or if the vehicle ahead is travelling only slightly slower than you want to go, the answer is probably 'no'.
Is it legal?	In particular, check the road markings. Never cross a continuous white line, except in an emergency. And don't overtake if you would need to exceed the speed limit to do so.
Is it safe?	Make sure the road ahead is clear and you have enough room to overtake and return to your own side of the road. Overtaking a long vehicle while going uphill in a fully loaded truck might take longer than you think. If in doubt, don't do it. Also make sure that the location is safe – for example, don't overtake at a humpbacked bridge, or at a turn or dip in the road.

To overtake safely, you need to be able to judge the speed of your truck relative to that of the vehicle you want to overtake and to that of other vehicles – including those coming against you. Don't ever 'take a chance'. Make sure you use your mirrors before, during and after overtaking.

Overtaking on the left

You must normally overtake on the right. However, you are allowed to overtake on the left in the following situations:

- You want to go straight ahead, when the driver in front of you has moved out and signalled that they intend to turn right;
- You have signalled that you intend to turn left; or
- Traffic in both lanes is moving slowly and traffic in the left-hand lane is moving more quickly than the traffic in the right-hand lane.

My commitment: 12
I am able to overtake slower-moving vehicles, and do so only when it is necessary, legal and safe.
Signed (Learner)

Starting on a hill

Starting your truck on a hill, facing up or down, is an important skill to master. To do this you need at all times to maintain control of the truck (having selected the appropriate gear) with precise and coordinated use of the clutch, accelerator, brake and handbrake.

Initially, practise starting on hills (up and down) on gentle slopes and with the support of your ADI.

My commitment: 13
I am able to coordinate and control precisely the clutch, accelerator and handbrake; and I am able to start the truck safely on a hill – both downhill and uphill.
Signed (Learner)

Údarás Um Shábháilteacht Ar Bhóithre
Road Safety Authority

Preparing for the unexpected

In your general driving practice, you need to always expect the unexpected. You literally don't know what's around the next bend, but you can avoid some dangerous situations by developing your observation skills and learning to anticipate danger. Even the best and safest drivers, however, will have to make emergency stops from time to time.

The quicker you respond to a potential emergency, the more likely you are to avert it. So, keep alert and be ready. In an emergency situation, your objective is to stop as quickly as possible while retaining control of the truck:

- If you brake too strongly, the truck may skid out of control; and
- If you don't brake strongly enough, the truck won't stop in time.

Keep both hands on the steering wheel while you are braking – all your concentration must go on controlling the truck and bringing it safely to a stop.

My commitment: 14
I will always drive in a safe and responsible manner, and try to anticipate danger.
Signed (Learner)

Driving on motorways

You may drive on a motorway only in a class of vehicle for which you have a full licence. So, to drive a truck on a motorway, you must have a full truck licence in the appropriate category – full C licence to drive a category C truck, full EC licence to drive a category EC truck and so on.

The *Rules of the Road* gives comprehensive guidance on motorway driving and also shows examples of the advance signs and warning signs you will meet on the motorway.

Dealing with fast-moving traffic

Motorways are designed so that traffic can move very freely and at higher speeds than on ordinary national routes (N-roads). They are built to accommodate large vehicles and are generally safer to drive on.

Driving a large vehicle in fast-moving traffic in multiple lanes requires total concentration and keen observation. Even the slightest distraction can have very serious consequences.

Motorway driving can also be very monotonous and tiring, and tiredness is a major contributor to motorway collisions. Make sure you are well-rested before starting a long motorway journey, and open the window a little every now and then to let in some fresh air.

What lane to drive in

You must not drive a type of vehicle that is restricted to a maximum vehicle speed limit of 80km/h or less in the traffic lane nearest the centre median of the motorway (the outside lane). An exception to this prohibition applies at any location where the speed limit is 80km/h or less.

Knowing where you're going

When you are intending to travel on a motorway you need to prepare your route much more carefully than you would on N-roads or regional roads. Keep in mind that you can't stop and ask for directions on a motorway.

Which exit to take

When you are on the motorway, you need to know which exit to take and you need to get into the correct lane well in advance of the exit. For example, if you are travelling from Portlaoise to Kildare, you leave the M7 at junction 13. Advance information is posted at 2-kilometre and 1-kilometre points before each junction.

Getting onto the motorway

Finding your way around motorway junctions can be quite confusing and you can easily lose bearings. On slip roads, in particular, you might have the feeling that you are going around in circles. For that reason you need to study the direction signs much more carefully than on N-roads, and you need to know the outline of your route in advance.

Motorway end points

You also need to know the end point of the motorway you are travelling on. For example, if you are travelling from Thurles to Clonmel, you join the M8 near Cashel and follow the signs for Cork (not Dublin). Clonmel will not be signposted until you get closer to the exit that leads to Clonmel – junction 10, near Cahir.

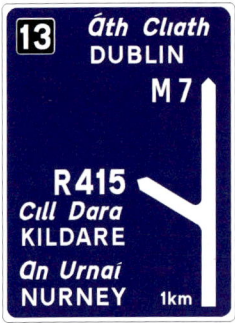

This advance direction sign shows that the turn-off for Kildare and Nurney is 1 kilometre away.

Points of the compass

In some cases, directions are indicated as points of the compass, so you need to know which direction you are going in.

- For example, if you are travelling from Finglas to Drogheda, you join the M50 at Finglas by taking the access road marked M50–**Northbound** Dublin Port.
- Similarly, if you are travelling from Finglas to Bray, you join the M50 at Finglas by taking the access road marked M50–**Southbound** Dún Laoghaire.

Getting help with route planning

The Ordnance Survey publishes a range of maps and atlases, including the *Official Road Atlas Ireland*. There are also many online resources that you can use to help you find the best route to where you want to go.

My commitment: 15

I hold a full truck driving licence, have practised motorway driving and understand the challenges that it presents; and in particular, I appreciate the concentration required to drive for prolonged periods at higher speed. I understand the importance of good route planning in advance of beginning a motorway journey.

Signed (Learner)

4. Complying with regulations

In this chapter

Truck drivers are required to comply with a number of regulations in addition to those that apply to drivers of cars or vans.

These regulations relate mainly to the health and safety of drivers and to the roadworthiness of vehicles being used on public roads. This chapter describes:

- The number of hours that a truck driver is allowed to drive each day and each week, and the minimum time off that a truck driver must take;
- How to comply with the regulations about tachographs;
- How to obtain a Certificate of Roadworthiness for your truck;
- How to obtain a Road Haulage Operator's Licence;
- Regulations relating to the carriage of dangerous materials; and
- Regulations relating to the transport of wide or abnormal loads.

Drivers' hours

For all professional drivers of goods vehicles over 3.5 tonnes (including trailers), the EU sets out detailed rules relating to drivers' hours, breaks and rest periods. The purpose of these rules is to improve drivers' working conditions and to contribute to road safety by reducing the risk of drivers becoming fatigued.

How long can you drive for?

The rules relating to driving time are:

- The maximum length of time you can drive without a break is 4½ hours. After that you must take a break of at least 45 minutes. Alternatively, you can take a break of 30 minutes at the end, provided you have previously taken a break of at least 15 minutes at some stage during (but not before) the 4½ hour driving period.
- You must not drive for more than 9 hours a day or 56 hours a week. The daily limit may be increased to 10 hours for two days a week. But you may not drive for more than 90 hours in any two-week period. So, if you drive for 56 hours in the first week of a two-week period, then you may drive for no more than 34 hours in the second week.

What is a break?

A break is a period during which you may not carry out any other work, such as loading and unloading, cleaning, technical maintenance, and so on. Breaks are to be used exclusively for rest and recuperation.

Combining driving and other work

When you combine driving with other work, such as loading and unloading, maintenance or administrative work, the following rules apply:

- You may not work for more than 6 hours without taking a break;
- If you work for between 6 and 9 hours you must take a break of at least 30 minutes at some stage during that period.
- If you work for more than 9 hours you must take a break of at least 45 minutes at some stage during that period.

Within these working periods, however, the maximum allowed driving time (aggregated) without a break is 4½ hours. For example, if you alternate between driving and unloading/delivering, you must record each of the driving periods. The aggregate of the driving periods must not exceed 4½ hours before you take a break, and the break must be of at least 45 minutes.

Shift example 1: one 45-minute break

Activity	Times
Other (checking etc.)	7.30– 8.00 (30 mins)
Driving	8.00 – 12.15 (4 hrs 15 mins)
Break	12.15 – 13.00 (45 mins)
Driving	13.00 – 16.00 (3 hrs)
Other (admin.)	16.00 – 16.15 (15 mins)

In this example, the driver begins the day checking the truck. He then drives for 4¼ hours. At 12.15 he takes a 45-minute break and then drives for another 3 hours. At the end of the day, he spends 15 minutes on administrative work.

Total working time:	8 hrs
Total driving time:	7 hrs 15 mins
Total break time:	45 mins

Shift example 2: split break

Activity	Times
Other (checking etc.)	7.30 – 8.00 (30 mins)
Driving	8.00 – 10.00 (2 hrs)
Break	10.00 – 10.15 (15 mins)
Driving	10.15 – 12.45 (2 hrs 30 mins)
Break	12.45 – 13.15 (30 mins)
Driving	13.15 – 16.30 (3 hrs 15 mins)
Other (admin.)	16.30 – 16.45 (15 mins)

In this example, the driver begins the day by checking the truck. She then drives for 2 hours. At 10.00 she takes a 15-minute break, and then continues driving for 2½ hours.

At 12.45 she takes a 30-minute break; and then drives for 3¼ hours. She ends the day with 15 minutes of administrative work and cleaning.

Total working time:	8 hrs 30 mins
Total driving time:	7 hrs 45 mins
Total break time:	45 mins

Shift example 3: two deliveries, with one 45-minute break

Activity	Times
Other (checking etc.)	7.30 – 8.00 (30 mins)
Driving	8.00 – 10.00 (2 hrs)
Other (delivering)	10.00 – 10.30 (30 mins)
Driving	10.30 – 13.00 (2 hrs 30 mins)
Break	13.00 – 13.45 (45 mins)
Other (delivering)	13.30 – 14.00 (30 mins)
Driving	14.00 – 16.00 (2 hrs)
Other (admin.)	16.00 – 16.15 (15 mins)

In this example, the driver begins the day by checking the truck and supervising loading. During the morning he makes a delivery which takes 30 minutes. By 13.00 he has worked for 5½ hours of which 4½ hours have been driving time. So, he is now required to take a 45-minute break.

After the break he makes a delivery (30 minutes) and then drives for 2 hours. He ends the day by spending 15 minutes on administrative work.

Total working time:	8 hrs 15 mins
Total driving time:	6 hrs 30 mins
Total break time:	45 mins

Shift example 4: single delivery, with one 45-minute break

Activity	Times
Other (checking etc.)	8.00 – 8.30 (30 mins)
Driving	8.30 – 12.30 (4 hrs)
Other (delivering)	12.30 – 13.30 (1 hr)
Break	13.30 – 14.15 (45 mins)
Driving	14.15 – 16.15 (2 hrs)
Other (admin etc.)	16.15 – 16.45 (30 mins)

The driver spends the morning loading, driving and delivering. By 13.30 she has worked for 5½ hours without a break. Of this period, 4 hours have been driving time – in other words, she is very close to the 4½ hour maximum driving time.

So, it is better to take the break now, rather than driving on for the maximum further allowed time of 30 minutes without a break.

After taking the 45-minute break, she's back on the road for 2 hours, and at the end of the day she spends 30 minutes on administrative work and cleaning.

Total working time:	8 hrs
Total driving time:	6 hrs
Total break time:	45 mins

Shift example 5: shorter driving time, with one 30-minute break

Activity	Times
Other (checking etc.)	8.00 – 8.30 (30 mins)
Driving	8.30 – 9.00 (30 mins)
Other (loading)	9.00 – 12.00 (3 hrs)
Driving	12.00 – 12.30 (30 mins)
Other (delivering)	12.30 – 14.00 (1 hr 30 mins)
Break	14.00 – 14.30 (30 mins)
Driving	14.30 – 16.30 (2 hrs)
Other (admin.)	16.30 – 16.45 (15 mins)

The driver spends most of the working day loading and delivering. By 14.00, however, he has worked for 6 hours and is required to take a break of at least 30 minutes.

The aggregate driving time for the day amounts to a total of 3 hours, which is less than the 4½ hour maximum driving time without a break.

Total working time:	8 hrs 15 mins
Total driving time:	3 hrs
Total break time:	30 mins

How much rest to take

There are also rules on how much rest you should take, every day and every week. Rest means that you are free to use your time as you wish – you may not do any form of work during your rest time.

Daily rest

You must take a daily rest period of at least 11 hours. You may take your rest time as:

- An uninterrupted period of at least 11 hours; or
- A split rest in two periods – an uninterrupted period of at least 3 hours and a second uninterrupted period of at least 9 hours. If you take this option, the total daily rest is at least 12 hours.

You may opt to take a reduced daily rest period of between 9 hours and 11 hours, but you may do so no more than twice in a week.

Daily rest when journey involves transport by ferry or train

In cases where your truck is being transported by ferry or train, you may interrupt your daily rest to drive the truck vehicle on or off the ferry or train, provided that:

- There are no more than two such interruptions and the total time taken does not exceed one hour;
- You have access to a bunk or couchette during the rest period; and
- The total rest period you take is at least 11 hours – in other words, you may not interrupt a reduced daily rest period in this way.

For shorter ferry crossings or train journeys, you may choose to regard the time you spend on the ferry or train as a break and not as a daily rest period.

Weekly rest

A period of 45 hours is regarded as the normal weekly rest; and a period of at least 24 hours is regarded as a reduced weekly rest. In any two consecutive weeks you must take either:

- Two normal breaks of 45 hours; or
- One normal rest break of 45 hours and one reduced rest of no less than 24 hours.

Compensation for reduced rest period

If you take a reduced weekly rest period, you must be compensated for the hours you have not taken. This compensation must be taken before the end of the third week after the week in which you take the reduced rest period. The compensation rest is added to another daily or weekly rest period of at least nine hours.

Example of weekly rest

Week 1	Week 2	Week 3	Week 4
35 hours' weekly rest (reduced weekly rest period)	45 hours' weekly rest (regular rest period)	45 hours' weekly rest (regular rest period)	45 hours' weekly rest *plus* compensation of 10 hours from week 1

In this example, Week 4 is the third week after Week 1, in which the driver took a reduced weekly rest period of 35 hours.

When does weekly rest start?

Your weekly rest period must start no later than 6 days after your previous weekly rest period. For example, if you finish your weekly rest period at 08.00 on Monday, your next weekly rest period must begin by 08.00 on the following Sunday.

Weekly rest period in the vehicle

You may not take regular weekly rest periods in a vehicle. You may, however, take daily rest periods and reduced weekly rest periods away from base in a vehicle. The vehicle must be stationary during the rest periods and must be fitted with suitable sleeping facilities for you and any other driver.

See also

The RSA website has detailed information on the regulations governing drivers' hours. See under **Professional Drivers**.

My commitment: 16

As a professional truck driver, I appreciate the importance of the regulations relating to drivers' hours and daily and weekly rest.

I will always comply with these regulations – as a contribution both to road safety and to my own health and working conditions.

Signed (Learner)

Tachographs

Under EU and national law, the cabs of trucks and buses must be fitted with a recording device known as a tachograph. Its function is to record information on a range of vehicle and driver activities. Driver activity includes driving time, rest, breaks, other work, and periods of availability. Vehicle information includes details of vehicle speed and distance travelled.

Data for all drivers of the vehicle is stored in the unit's memory. Each individual driver must have their own Digital Tachograph Driver Card that records their own activity. Older vehicles have analogue tachographs that record data on a circular chart.

Applying for a Digital Tachograph Driver Card

To drive a truck fitted with a digital tachograph, you are required by law to have a Digital Tachograph Driver Card. Application forms for these are available for download from the **Professional Drivers** section of the RSA website.

Enforcement of tachograph rules

The data on your Digital Tachograph Driver Card is your record of your driving time and rest time. An enforcement officer may ask you to produce your Driver Card and any manual record and print-out made during the current day and the previous 28 days. If you have driven a vehicle with an analogue tachograph within the last 28 days, you must also be able to produce the analogue charts recording your activities.

Tachograph guidelines

- Use the Driver Card every day you drive, starting from the moment you take over the vehicle.
- Set the mode switch to the correct activity and make sure to use it throughout your working period to record other work, periods of availability, rests and breaks.
- Remove your Driver Card when the vehicle is taken over by another driver, or when the vehicle is not under your custody or if another driver could drive it.
- Protect your Driver Card, keep it clean and do not bend it.
- Record the country in which you begin and end your daily work period. Do this always at the start and end of the period.
- Manually enter any non-driving activities since you last removed your driver card from a tachograph. This could include other work, breaks, rest and periods of availability.
- If you are driving a vehicle with an analogue tachograph, make sure to record your hours on an analogue chart, and make sure that your details and those of the truck are correct and up to date.

See also

The RSA has published a number of documents relating to tachographs, and these are all available on the RSA website – see under **Professional Drivers**. You can also download an application form for a Digital Tachograph Driver Card from the RSA website.

Tachograph training is available from a number of training companies, institutions and professional bodies. A typical introductory course to digital tachographs takes half a day.

My commitment: 17

I am competent in the use of a tachograph.

As a professional truck driver, I will maintain correct and up-to-date tachograph records at all times.

Signed (Learner)

Certificate of Roadworthiness

All commercial vehicles (and trailers) over one year old must have an up-to-date Certificate of Roadworthiness. To get a Certificate of Roadworthiness, a truck or trailer must pass the Commercial Vehicle Test. This test is a preventative road safety measure to ensure that all Irish HGVs are maintained to a minimum standard of roadworthiness.

Vehicles that pass the Commercial Vehicle Test are awarded a pass statement, which can be exchanged for a Certificate of Roadworthiness at any Motor Tax Office. An up-to-date certificate is proof that your vehicle has been tested for roadworthiness and, as such, is viewed by the authorities as just as important as having valid tax and insurance.

Failure to have a current Certificate of Roadworthiness is an offence under Section 18 of the Road Traffic Act 1961. Conviction for this offence carries 5 penalty points and the courts may impose a fine and/or a prison sentence.

See also

The RSA website has detailed information on the regulations governing the Certificate of Roadworthiness.

Go to the **Professional Drivers** section of the RSA website and click on **Vehicle testing**.

Road Haulage Operator's Licence

You need a Road Haulage Operator's Licence to carry goods for reward for any trade or business in a vehicle of over 3.5 tonnes on a public road, and the vehicle must display an up-to-date Transport Disc as proof that it is licensed.

This applies to the owner of the vehicle used for carrying goods for reward. Drivers employed on contract by haulage companies should satisfy themselves that the contractor has a valid Road Haulage Operator's Licence for the vehicle and should check that the licence and Transport Disc are up to date.

A Road Haulage Operator's Licence is not necessary to:

- Carry livestock, milk or milk containers (to or from a creamery) and newly-harvested grain; or
- Carry on 'own account' work only. 'Own account' work is carriage of your own goods in your own vehicles driven by yourself or your employees, or the delivery of goods to a customer who has bought those goods from you.

See also

You can apply for a Road Haulage Operator's Licence to the Department of Transport at:

Road Transport Operator Licensing Unit
Department of Transport
Clonfert House
Bride Street
Loughrea, Co. Galway

Telephone:	LoCall 1890-443311 or 01-6707444
Fax:	091-872999
E-mail:	rtol@transport.ie

Carrying hazardous materials

There are strict EU regulations in place relating to the transport of hazardous goods by road. These govern both the vehicles used for transporting hazardous goods and the driver. The are usually referred to as ADR regulations – these are the initials of a French phrase meaning 'European agreement concerning international transport of dangerous goods by road' (Accord européen relatif au transport international des marchandises dangereuses par route).

Vehicle ADR

Any vehicle that transports dangerous goods is required by law to meet certain detailed technical requirements and it must have an ADR certificate.

See also

The RSA website has detailed information on the regulations governing ADR vehicle licensing.

Go to the **Vehicles & Legislation** section of the RSA website and click on **Heavy Goods Vehicles** and then on **Carrying dangerous goods** (ADR).

Driver ADR

Any driver who transports dangerous goods must have an ADR Driver Training Certificate. The Health & Safety Authority (HSA) administers the licensing of drivers in ADR.

See also

The HSA's website (www.hsa.ie) has detailed information on all aspects of how to get an ADR Driver Training Certificate.

Wide and abnormal loads

What is an abnormal load?

A load is considered 'abnormal' if it exceeds the regulation limits – these are the maximum weight or dimensions specified in the Road Traffic (Construction and Use of Vehicles) Regulations, 2003 (S.I. No. 5 of 2003).

See also

The regulation limits on the size of vehicles and loads are summarised in the RSA's *Guidelines on Maximum Weight and Dimensions of Mechanically Propelled Vehicles and Trailers*.

To access the *Guidelines*, enter guidelines weight dimensions in the Search box on the RSA website's home page (www.rsa.ie).

For a vehicle or load that exceeds these limits, you will need to obtain one or more permits. There are two kinds of permit:

- A **Garda permit** is required where:
  - The vehicle and load does not exceed 27.4 metres in length *or* 4.3 metres in width *or* 4.65 metres in height; *and*
  - The journey will take place entirely on designated roads (see below).
- In all other circumstances, a **local authority permit** is required for each local authority area through which you will pass.

Designated roads

The RSA website has a list and a map of designated roads. These are updated frequently as more roads come under the Garda scheme: enter designated roads in the Search box on the RSA website's home page (www.rsa.ie). Designated roads include many national roads (N-roads) and motorways.

Obtaining a Garda permit

Application forms for a Garda permit are available from the RSA's website and from An Garda Síochána's website (enter abnormal loads in the Search box). The application must be submitted at least five working days before the proposed journey.

There is no charge for permits issued under this scheme.

Obtaining a local authority permit

Local authorities (county and city councils) operate a permit system for all roads, vehicles and loads not covered under the Garda permit scheme. The requirements and charges for this scheme may vary from one local authority to another, so you should contact the relevant local authority before you apply.

You need a permit from each local authority through whose area the vehicle will travel. For example, if you are travelling from Killybegs to Ballina, you will need permits from the county councils in Donegal, Leitrim, Sligo and Mayo.

See also

For contact details for all the local authorities (county and city councils) see:

http://www.environ.ie/en/LocalGovernment/LocalGovernmentAdministration/LocalAuthorities/

Summary of permit requirements

Size of vehicle/load	Journey details	Permit requirements
The vehicle/load is: ○ longer than 27.4 metres; or ○ wider than 4.3 metres; or; ○ higher than 4.65 metres	Any journey	You must have: ○ A local authority permit for each local authority area you pass through.
The vehicle/load exceeds the regulation limits but is *not*: ○ longer than 27.4 metres; or ○ wider than 4.3 metres; or; ○ higher than 4.65 metres	The journey takes place entirely on designated roads	You must have: ○ A Garda permit.
	The journey is partly on roads designated under the Garda scheme	You must have: ○ *For the part of the journey that takes place on designated roads:* a Garda permit; and ○ *For the part of the journey that takes place on non-designated roads:* local authority permits for each local authority area through which the vehicle/load will travel.
	The journey takes place entirely on non-designated roads	You must have: ○ Local authority permits for each local authority area through which the vehicle/load will travel.

5. Dealing with more challenging conditions

In this chapter

This chapter looks at some of the more challenging conditions that you will face as a truck driver. Most of these are conditions that you will need to learn about at first hand – including driving in heavy traffic, driving at night and in bad weather. Other conditions, such as heavy snow or ice, are not that common in Ireland, but you need to know how to handle them when you come across them.

In the course of your practice journeys with your ADI, you will sometimes come across challenging conditions without warning. For example, there might be a sudden downpour or you might find yourself in traffic coming from a sporting event you didn't know about. In such conditions, the important thing is to keep up the good habits you have already learnt, and just apply them to the changed circumstances. The key skills of observation, judgement, planning and reaction still apply.

Combinations of challenging conditions

Challenging conditions can become even more difficult when they come in combination – for example, driving at night in very heavy rain on a very busy national road. Usually, when driving conditions are challenging, you will need to reduce your speed and be even more careful to observe what's going on.

Dealing with hazards

A hazard is anything that means you might have to change the position, speed or direction of your vehicle. For example, a road feature such as a sharp bend could be a hazard, and so could the actions of other road users.

As you build up experience of a wide variety of road and traffic conditions, you will become better at scanning the road ahead. This will help you to further develop the essential skills of observation, judgement, planning and reaction. The rest of this chapter deals with challenging conditions where you need to make use of these skills.

Driving in heavy traffic

Driving in heavy traffic is not a very pleasant experience. You have to drive a lot slower than normal, and it takes longer to get to where you're going. You use up a lot more fuel stopping and moving off, and you have less road space in which to manoeuvre. Also, traffic conditions are unpredictable, which can lead to unexpected delays and frustration. You need to learn how to anticipate and react to changing traffic conditions.

Why is driving in heavy traffic challenging?

In heavy traffic you are likely to be driving at low speeds, and stopping and starting quite a lot – this brings with it a number of challenges. Keep in mind that:

- Your pedal control needs to be very precise – your left foot will spend quite a lot of time on the clutch or hovering just above it;
- You could be 'surrounded' in a middle lane with vehicles, perhaps other trucks or buses, on both sides;
- Bicycles and motorcycles may pass on either side of you;
- Each vehicle has less road space around it in heavy traffic and manoeuvring a truck can be more difficult; and
- Changing lane can be very difficult – you are relying on the courtesy of drivers in other lanes to let you change.

Other drivers: risks and intimidation

In heavy, slow-moving traffic, some drivers get frustrated – they're late for work or for an appointment, or they just want to get home. Research shows that the highest number of traffic collisions happen during the evening rush, between 4 and 6 o'clock, when traffic is at its heaviest.

The biggest challenges you are likely to face in heavy traffic come from other drivers:

- Some drivers may take unnecessary risks, such as changing lanes very suddenly or taking a chance at a level crossing. You need to stay very alert for such behaviour; and
- Other drivers may try to intimidate you in various ways.

My commitment: 18
I have practised driving a truck in heavy traffic. I am confident that I can control the truck, remain patient, and deal with the frustrations of being stuck in traffic.
Signed (Learner)

Night-time driving

Why is driving at night challenging?

Your skills of observation depend on what you can actually see, and also on your perception of how far away or how near things are, on your perception of the speed of other vehicles relative to yours, on differences in colour and light, and on your peripheral vision. At night you have much less evidence upon which to base the judgements you make and the actions you take while driving. This is especially the case with driving on unlit rural roads.

Tiredness and other factors at night

You're also more likely to be tired at night, and this will also affect your observation skills as well as your reaction times. There are other factors that can make driving at night challenging. Keep in mind that:

- Traffic is generally much lighter at night, and some drivers are tempted to drive faster than they ought to;
- At night you are much more likely to be sharing the road with drivers whose behaviour is affected by alcohol or fatigue; and
- You can be dazzled both by oncoming and following drivers who don't dip their main headlights. Even if you're not dazzled, driving against a steady stream of traffic with dipped lights can be very tiring and a strain on your eyes which are constantly adjusting between darkness and very bright light.

Some tips for driving safely at night

About a third of all serious road collisions take place at night. This is a very high proportion considering the relatively low volumes of traffic on the roads at night. For that reason alone, you need to pay extra attention when driving at night, particularly while you are learning.

- You don't necessarily have to drive slower at night, but you do need to moderate your speed to allow for the fact that your perception of possible hazards is limited. If you don't think you could safely bring the truck to a stop within the range of what you can see with your dipped headlights, then you're travelling too fast – slow down!
- Driving at night presents special challenges, especially in unlit places. Headlights from oncoming vehicles can really affect your night vision. Slow down, maintain a safe course, and avoid looking directly into the headlights of oncoming vehicles. It might take your eyes some time to adjust to different light conditions.
- Think of other drivers and dip your main lights when you see the lights of an oncoming vehicle. You should also dip your lights when you are following another vehicle, to avoid causing mirror dazzle. If you suspect that your lights are not correctly aligned (in other words that even with dipped headlights you are still dazzling oncoming vehicles), have them checked by a mechanic.
- If you do not already have your dipped headlights on, turn them on at dusk – don't wait for total darkness to fall. This will help other road users to see you.
- It is important that all lights and reflectors are clean and in working order at all times, but this is especially important at night.
- Poor night vision can be a serious hazard. Symptoms include difficulty seeing when driving in the evening or at night, poor vision in reduced light, and feeling that the eyes take longer to 'adjust' to seeing in the dark. If you have concerns about your night vision, seek medical advice.
- Auxiliary lights (extra lights such as fog lights and spot lights) should be used only when appropriate and legal.

The *Rules of the Road* gives detailed advice on driving at night.

Driving in rural areas at night

When driving at night in unlit rural areas, use full beam headlights to give yourself the best view of the road ahead. Make sure to dip your headlights when:

- You meet an oncoming vehicle or other road users; or
- You are following another vehicle – your full beams reflecting in the mirror of the vehicle in front can be very dazzling.

Overtaking at night

Avoid overtaking at night unless it's necessary. Take extra care when doing so, as reduced visibility makes it more difficult to judge speed and distance.

My commitment: 19

I have practised driving at night on a variety of different roads, urban and rural. I understand the particular dangers of driving at night and will always drive with consideration for other road users.

Signed (Learner)

Driving in conditions of poor visibility

Any kind of weather that makes it more difficult for you to see what's happening on the road (and makes it more difficult for other road users to see you) presents particular driving challenges.

Driving in heavy rain

In very heavy rain (or falling snow, hailstones or sleet) your visibility is considerably reduced. You're looking at the road through a continuous sheet of rain, your wipers are sweeping back and forth, and the cold air outside is likely to cause your windows to mist up. You also have to cope with splashes or spray from other vehicles. And at night time the wet road surface reflects the lights of oncoming vehicles and causes glare.

In addition to poor visibility, you need to be aware that a wet road surface does not give your tyres the same level of grip as a dry surface. The road might be particularly slippery when it gets wet after a long spell of dry weather.

What is aquaplaning?

Aquaplaning happens when a vehicle is being driven on a wet road, and a film of water builds up between the tyres and the road surface, so that the tyres are not in direct contact with the road surface.

When the vehicle aquaplanes, the steering will seem very 'loose'. Stay calm, ease off the accelerator to slow down, but avoid braking if possible. At a slower speed the water will be dispersed and the tyres will regain their grip on the road surface.

What can you do?

There are a number of things you can do to help make driving safer in heavy rain (or falling snow, hailstones or sleet).

- Turn on your headlights (dipped) so that other drivers can see you more easily.
- Slow down and stay further back from the vehicle in front of you, especially if this is a bus or another truck that is making a lot of spray. You still need to keep up with the general flow of traffic, but bear in mind that your stopping distance is much greater on wet, greasy roads.
- Be considerate in how you treat other road users in very heavy rain. At least you're inside and dry – pedestrians, cyclists and motorcyclists are not so lucky. Keep in mind that:
  - A pedestrian with an umbrella facing into the wind might not see traffic, and the noise of the rain might also drown out the sound of traffic;
  - When approaching pedestrians and cyclists you should be careful not to splash them as you pass; and
  - Cyclists and motorcyclists also have very limited vision in heavy rain and their safe stopping distances are also much greater. Take into account that bicycle brakes don't work very well in wet conditions.
- Brake earlier and more gently than you normally would.

Localised flooding

When you have driven through a large puddle or localised flooding, your brakes may become less effective. Test your brakes to ensure that they have not been affected by the water – check in your mirrors before you do this.

If they have been affected (and this is more than likely just temporary) and if it is safe, press gently on the brake pedal as you are driving until they dry out and return to normal.

 The RSA recommends the use of daytime running lights (where fitted) or dipped headlights during daylight conditions.

Driving into a low sun

We usually associate poor visibility with bad weather, but good weather can also cause problems. In particular, you can be dazzled when driving into a low sun (particularly in winter). Keep a pair of sunglasses handy in the cab, and use the sun visor to shade your eyes.

If you usually wear glasses or contact lenses, consider getting sunglasses to suit your prescription.

The build-up of 'traffic film' on the inside of the windscreen can make it even harder to see when driving into a low sun. Keep the inside and outside of the windscreen clean to avoid the risk of being dazzled.

Driving in fog

Fog is one of the most dangerous weather conditions for all kinds of transport. In dense fog, airports close down and ships stay in port. On the roads, fog can range from being a minor nuisance to being a serious danger.

What can you do?

Driving in dense fog is not recommended, and you should not travel in foggy conditions unless you really have to. Fog, however, is often quite localised and can come down suddenly without warning. You need to be prepared for it and to know how to behave if you do find yourself driving in fog. There are a number of things you can do to help make driving in fog safer:

- Make sure to stay a safe distance from the vehicle in front of you, and be satisfied at all times that you can stop within the distance that you can see to be clear.
- Drive at a steady, slow speed. Fog is usually patchy and you will pass through areas where visibility varies. Don't be tempted to speed up through the good patches, as you might find yourself all of a sudden in another dense patch. (Most motorway pile-ups happen when vehicles are driving too fast and too close together.)
- Make sure that other road users can see you. Turn on your headlights (dipped) and fog lights. Don't turn on your main beam headlights, as these just beam into the fog and make it more difficult to see where you're going. If the fog is dense, turn on rear fog lights if you have them – but remember to turn them off when the fog is gone.

My commitment: 20

I have practised driving in conditions of poor daytime visibility. I appreciate the importance of seeing and being seen.

Signed (Learner)

Údarás Um Shábháilteacht Ar Bhóithre
Road Safety Authority

Driving in poor on-road conditions

In conditions where the road is covered with snow or ice, or is flooded or has patches of loose gravel, your grip on the road can be impaired. In these conditions you are more likely to lose control of the truck, especially at higher speeds.

Snow and ice

Snow and ice can make driving very hazardous, and you should avoid making any unnecessary journeys in snow or icy conditions or if these are forecast. If you're not sure, listen to radio broadcasts or warnings from the Road Safety Authority.

Snow and icy conditions can arrive quite suddenly, and you might find yourself driving in snow or ice without expecting to.

Fresh snow

Freshly fallen snow is not as slippery on the road as ice or compacted snow. Moderate your speed and keep a good distance from the vehicle in front.

Be aware, however, that fresh snow will cover the road markings and catseyes, including those that mark the edge and the middle of the road. If you are the first vehicle to drive on the fresh snow, you might have difficulty knowing where you are on the road. This will be less of a problem in urban areas where roadside buildings and street furniture will guide you or on busier roads where you can follow the tyre tracks of vehicles that have gone before you.

Where snow is accompanied by strong winds, be mindful that the snow might drift and be much deeper in certain places. Listen to broadcast warnings, and do not drive on roads where snow drifts are reported.

You should also watch out for roadside warning signs that might be covered with snow and become more difficult to read. STOP and YIELD signs have distinctive shapes (octagonal and triangular respectively) for that reason.

Ice and compacted snow

Where there is ice or compacted snow on the road, you need to drive with extreme caution and keep your distance from the vehicle ahead – even where the road has been gritted and salted by the local authority. Your safe stopping distance can be up to ten times greater on an icy surface than on a normal dry one.

Compacted snow that has frozen overnight is particularly treacherous and as it thaws it becomes even more slippery and dangerous. In such conditions, some roads become impassable – for example those with steep hills or with humpbacked bridges.

Údarás Um Shábháilteacht Ar Bhóithre
Road Safety Authority

Driving through the thaw

As weather conditions improve after a period of snow and frost, it's easy to become complacent, but there are a number of things you should look out for:

- There will be sheltered areas with patches of melting ice that are still very slippery – for example, at bends in the road with overhanging bushes;
- There is a risk of skidding on loose grit spread by the local authorities;
- Melting snow and ice may lead to localised flooding;
- The road surface might have been damaged by the snow and ice, so you need to be on the lookout for potholes and other hazards; and
- Where there is a build-up of slush and ice at the sides of the road, cyclists and motorcyclists may have to travel closer to the centre of the road than usual.

Black ice

Black ice is an almost invisible, thin coating of ice on the road surface. It is particularly dangerous because it is hard to see. When the temperature drops close to freezing you can expect to find black ice – particularly in sheltered or shaded areas of the roadway, under trees or beside high walls. Sometimes it can look like a sheet of water or as if the road is wet.

Snow and ice: general advice

- Listen to weather reports and forecasts – if the temperature is expected to drop close to or below freezing, then you will know to expect icy road conditions.
- Avoid driving in snowy or icy conditions unless you have to.
- Make sure your tyres have at least the minimum legal tread depth and are correctly inflated.
- On icy roads, your stopping distance can be up to ten times what it is normally, and it can be very difficult to control the truck as you brake. For that reason, you need to:
  - Slow down;
  - Keep your distance from the vehicle in front; and
  - Make sure that all your manoeuvres are smooth and gentle: brake gently and accelerate very gently.
- Drive in the highest possible gear – this will help you to avoid 'wheel spin'.
- If visibility is poor, turn on your dipped headlights.
- Keep yourself informed about road conditions in times of bad weather – see the RSA website for advice, and listen to radio traffic and weather updates.

Avoiding skids

The most common causes of a skid are driving too fast for the on-road conditions and jerky braking, gear changing or steering. You can reduce the likelihood of skidding by driving smoothly at an appropriate speed, and by keeping your distance from the vehicle in front. Don't rely on your ABS to prevent you from skidding – it won't always do so.

My commitment: 21

I appreciate the dangers of driving in snow and ice and I will not make any unnecessary journeys in such conditions. When I do drive in snow and ice I will drive slower, leave more room ahead, and accelerate and brake smoothly and gently.

Signed (Learner)

Driving in high winds

Driving a truck in high winds can be a very challenging experience, especially for high-sided or curtain-sided vehicles, which can be blown off course or (in extreme circumstances) blown over.

Be alert to crosswinds on exposed stretches of road, on elevated bridges, on the crests of hills, and whenever you see the Crosswinds alert sign. Depending on the type of load you are carrying, you might need to take extra precautions – for example:

- On curtain sided trucks, ensure that the straps are strongly secured and not likely to loosen;
- Where goods are secured by ropes and sheeting on an open truck, make sure that these are very secure and not likely to flap or loosen; and
- Cyclists and pedestrians are particularly vulnerable in very windy conditions – be particularly careful when overtaking them.

Dealing with road works and other obstructions

The National Roads Authority and local authorities around the country are continually working to provide a safe, efficient road network and to maintain the quality of road surfaces. Roadworks can vary – they could be major jobs or smaller works, and include the construction of new roads, emergency repairs, routine maintenance of fences and barriers, trimming hedgerows, clearing litter, cutting grass verges, and so on.

When you come across roadworks of any kind, you need to drive with extra care, for your own safety, the safety of other road users and the safety of the road workers.

Roadworks present challenges to all drivers, and you may come across some or all of the following conditions:

- Detours and different traffic patterns;
- Loose chippings;
- Different lane markers and traffic cones;
- Narrower lanes than usual and restricted shoulder areas;
- Unfinished or very uneven road surfaces;
- Large slow-moving works vehicles on the road;
- Stop–Go systems or temporary traffic lights; and
- Contraflows on motorways and dual carriageways.

Warning signs

The *Rules of the Road* lists warning signs relating to road works. These signs give warnings, advice and instructions, including information about speed restrictions, detours and road surface conditions. Make sure that you understand what all of these warning signs mean.

Staying safe at roadworks

Follow these easy guidelines to help maintain safety at road works sites:

- Slow down and obey the temporary speed limits posted;
- Obey all the signs, temporary traffic lights and any instructions given to you by flagmen and other road workers;
- Keep a safe distance from the vehicle in front;
- Follow the lane markers and cones (where present); and
- Be alert to the movements of road workers and of works traffic.

Údarás Um Shábháilteacht Ar Bhóithre
Road Safety Authority

My commitment: 22
I will always drive through road works with care and consideration, and I will obey the warning signs and any instructions the road workers give me.

Signed (Learner)

Town and country: challenges of urban and rural driving

Town and country driving each presents very different kinds of challenges to the truck driver. While you are practising, your journeys should cover both.

Town and city driving

Driving a truck in towns and cities presents you with a variety of difficult driving situations, often in very quick succession. By this stage in your driving progress you might be reasonably comfortable with complex junctions, multi-lane roundabouts and one-way systems. However, in towns and cities, you will come across these challenges much more often, and they are especially difficult if you are driving in heavy traffic. Hazards you need to be particularly careful about while driving in towns and cities include:

- Obstructions caused by vans and other trucks making deliveries;
- Buses pulling in and out at bus stops;
- Cars parked on the side of the street – be careful of doors opening unexpectedly or of children running out from between parked cars;
- More vulnerable road users to consider – including pedestrians and cyclists; and
- Stop-start driving – as the distance between junctions can be quite short.

In some areas there are restrictions on vehicles with 3 or 5 axles or more. Usually, the restrictions are for particular time periods. Local authorities have a permit system to enable vehicles that exceed these limits to be used to deliver or collect goods. For example, In most of central Dublin vehicles of 5 or more axles are not permitted between 7 am and 7 pm without a permit.

In many urban areas there are restrictions on where you can park a truck.

Urban speed limit

The general speed limit for built-up areas is 50km/h (this might be lower in some areas).

Because of all the hazards in the urban environment, it is particularly important for drivers to have enough time to react, and you should never exceed the speed limit.

My commitment: 23

I have practised driving on urban streets and understand the particular hazards I am likely to come across there. In towns and cities I will always drive within the urban speed limit.

Signed (Learner)

Rural driving

Outside of the major urban areas, Ireland has a relatively low density of population served by a very extensive network of roads. This presents particular challenges to drivers, with more collisions occurring on rural roads than on urban roads.

Some rural roads may be too narrow or may be unsuitable for large vehicles in other ways. In some cases an alternative route is suggested.

Other road users

On country roads you are more likely to meet slow-moving vehicles, such as tractors and other agricultural vehicles. Don't try to overtake these vehicles unless you have a clear view of the road ahead and the road is wide enough to overtake safely. Be patient: they are probably travelling only a very short distance. Many narrow country roads do not have central road markings and allow very little room for two vehicles to pass – particularly where one of the vehicles is a truck.

You are more likely to meet livestock on country roads. Be prepared to slow down or stop and don't do anything to frighten the animals.

Visibility

High or overhanging hedges and the winding nature of country roads can impair visibility – blind corners, sharp bends and dips in the road can be particularly dangerous. You should always adjust your speed to suit the road you are driving on and you must never exceed the speed limit. In many cases, a safe speed might be much less than the stated speed limit for the road. You need to be able to stop the truck in the road space that you can see – if you can't, you're driving too fast.

Make sure you heed warnings to slow down and warning signs for dangerous bends or corners.

Road surface

Local authorities give priority to maintaining roads with heavier traffic, so country roads with less traffic might not have the same surface quality. Also, on country roads watch out for loose gravel, mud and things like fallen leaves on the road – all of these can make the surface slippery, especially after rain.

My commitment: 24

I have practised driving on country roads and I understand that visibility might be poor and that the road surfaces might be more uneven than on urban or national roads. While driving on country roads I will be considerate to the needs of farmers and other country dwellers and their animals.

Signed (Learner)

6. Sharing the road

In this chapter

The basic skills of driving a truck will take you a while to master, and you will need a good ADI, and a well-planned schedule of driving practice. The most important skill to learn, however, is that of sharing the road responsibly with other people; to do this, you need to:

- Be in good physical and mental condition to drive safely and competently;
- Stay calm even if other drivers are behaving badly and not allow your own emotions to get the better of you;
- Avoid distractions while driving but learn to deal with those that do arise;
- Behave with consideration and courtesy towards other road users, including pedestrians, cyclists, motorcyclists, car drivers and other truck drivers;
- Consider how you can reduce the impact of your driving on the environment; and
- Know what to do if you arrive at the scene of a collision.

Making sure you're fit to drive

Medical conditions

Certain medical conditions can have an effect on driving. Even a bad cold or a simple viral infection can slow down your reaction time and lower your concentration levels. If you are currently being treated for any medical condition, ask your doctor if it is safe for you to drive.

Facts about alcohol

- Drink-driving is a factor in about a quarter of all fatal collisions in Ireland.
- Across Europe, alcohol or drugs are a factor in almost a quarter of all collisions, leading to about 10,000 deaths a year.

The effects of alcohol: never ever drink and drive

Driving while under the influence of alcohol puts you at a much greater risk of being involved in a collision. Collisions caused by drink-driving are usually preventable. **Never, ever drink and drive**. It's not worth the risk, either to yourself or to other road users.

Alcohol slows down your nervous system and causes you to function less effectively in many different ways. In summary, alcohol:

- Impairs your vision and reduces your 'field of vision' – in particular your peripheral vision (what you see out of the corner of your eye);
- Impairs your perception – your ability to judge how far away objects are, including other vehicles;
- Makes it more difficult for you to coordinate the various tasks that driving involves – steering, braking, observing road signs, and so on;
- Dulls your reflexes so that you are no longer able to react quickly in dangerous situations. In other words, your reaction time is much longer and your physical movements (for example, putting your foot on the brake) are much slower; and
- Causes loss of judgement, gives you false confidence and a lack of inhibition in relation to speed, which in turn leads to drivers 'taking a chance'.

The effects of other drugs

Drugs (legal and illegal) can impair your ability and change the way you drive. For example, drugs such as depressants dull your reactions, while stimulants heighten your senses and can make you overreact.

- Depressants (or downers) have similar effects to alcohol and are particularly dangerous when taken with alcohol. Prescribed depressants include tranquillisers for relief of anxiety and tension.
- Narcotics include some legally prescribed pain-killers and illegal drugs such as heroin and cannabis. Their effects include euphoria (feeling unnaturally happy), giddiness and drowsiness.
- Hallucinogenic drugs lead to nausea and affect your perception – which is especially dangerous considering how important perception is to a driver. This category of drugs includes Ecstasy and LSD.
- Stimulants are used medicinally to increase alertness and to relieve tiredness. They can also cause hyperactivity, aggressiveness and reckless behaviour – all of which impair your ability to drive safely.

If you are taking any kind of medication, prescribed or over-the-counter, ask your doctor or pharmacist to confirm that it's okay to drive.

The effects of tiredness

Fatigue – or tiredness – is one of the main causes of serious road collisions. When you're very tired, you are much less alert, have poorer physical coordination, and your reaction times are much slower. You will also find it more difficult to 'read the road' and take in direction signs, warning signs and other information as you drive. You also run the very grave risk of dozing off at the wheel, with potentially fatal consequences.

You are more likely to become tired when driving on main roads with low traffic volumes (particularly on motorways), where the driving task is monotonous and there is very little stimulation. Other conditions that can lead to tiredness include driving in:

- Traffic jams or very slow-moving traffic;
- Rain – when the windscreen wipers can have a hypnotic effect; or
- At night, when you would normally be asleep.

Avoiding and handling tiredness

The best way to handle tiredness is to avoid it in the first place – in particular, make sure you are well rested in advance of a longer journey. Tea or coffee can help some people, but do not depend on them to keep away tiredness. There are some things you can do to avoid and handle tiredness:

- Make sure that you always follow the daily and weekly rest regulations – see page 61.
- On longer trips, make sure that you always work within the Drivers' Hours rules and that you take adequate breaks.

My commitment: 25
I will drive only when I am physically fit to do so. I will never ever drink and drive. I will never ever drive while under the influence of drugs (legal or illegal). As a professional driver, I will always work within the Drivers' Hours rules and take adequate rest.
Signed (Learner)

Staying calm: showing courtesy

There are so many things that can stress you when you are driving: heavy traffic, bad weather, road works, waiting at level crossings, other drivers' bad behaviour – all of these can build up frustration and make it difficult to stay calm and focus on arriving safely at your destination. Your own emotional state can also play a big part in how well you drive. If you are worried or upset, angry or depressed, it will probably show in your driving.

You can help to reduce stress by giving yourself enough time to get to your destination without feeling rushed. Don't allow yourself to become impatient, as this can lead to rash behaviour and taking unnecessary risks. Stay courteous and tolerant in your dealings with other road users, particularly more vulnerable road users such as pedestrians and cyclists.

> **Annoying actions to avoid**
>
> Think about your own driving practice. Are there things you do that could annoy other drivers or other road users? The most common annoying actions (some of which are illegal) include:
> - Tailgating – driving too close to the vehicle in front;
> - Signalling late before turning – following vehicles might not be able to move around you;
> - Not dipping your main headlights when you meet oncoming vehicles;
> - Splashing cyclists and pedestrians;
> - Passing on the inside in fast-moving traffic;
> - Driving in the outer lane of a dual carriageway or motorway;
> - Aggressive use of the horn;
> - Weaving in and out of traffic lanes; and
> - Slowing down for no apparent reason or driving significantly below the speed limit for no good reason.

Other drivers' behaviour

Some drivers seem to think of driving as a kind of competitive sport, and don't have much consideration for other road users. They may cut inside you, indicate at the last minute, blare their horn, make aggressive gestures, and so on.

This kind of aggressive behaviour can very easily turn into 'road rage' where people who are normally civil and courteous lose self-control and act very irresponsibly when they feel themselves 'provoked'. Don't allow yourself to be drawn into this kind of situation. Let such drivers go ahead – you will be safer if you are not in their vicinity.

Good drivers stay patient, courteous and tolerant at all times and don't respond to provocation – they know that they'll get there just as quickly if they ignore such actions. If you find yourself in such a situation, 'count to ten' and give yourself time to cool down.

My commitment: 26

I understand the importance of remaining calm, patient and courteous at all times while driving.

I will not allow myself to be 'provoked' by the behaviour of other road users.

Signed (Learner)

Avoiding and dealing with distractions while driving

When you are driving you need to take in a great deal of information – about other traffic, road conditions, direction and warning signs, and so on. Just dealing with that amount of information is quite enough, and you don't need to add to the load by letting yourself be distracted. A distraction is anything that takes away your concentration while you are driving. If you are distracted, your reactions will be slower and your judgement will not be as good. It is an offence to drive 'without due care and attention'.

Mobile phones

Using a hand-held mobile phone while driving is an offence. It is unsafe because it prevents you from concentrating fully on driving. It is illegal to hold a mobile phone in your hand or to support it on your shoulder.

Using a hands-free phone kit is not illegal, but in some circumstances it could be a dangerous distraction, and you could be prosecuted for dangerous driving, careless driving or driving without due care and attention.

Maintaining concentration

Good truck drivers concentrate and keep their mind on the task in hand at all times. They don't allow distractions of any kind to interfere with their number one priority when driving – getting themselves and their goods to their destination safely. Things that can take from your concentration and distract your attention from the road include:

- Lighting and smoking cigarettes;
- Adjusting the radio tuner or CD player;
- Grooming activities;
- Using in-vehicle systems, such as multi-function displays;
- Programming a sat-nav; and
- Eating or drinking.

Dealing with other road users

As a truck driver you share the road with other drivers – of cars, buses and trucks – and with many other people as well: cyclists, motorcyclists, pedestrians, and in rural areas you can sometimes meet farm animals. You need to be conscious at all times of the different view of the road that other road users have. And you also need to understand your own responsibilities.

Pedestrians

Pedestrians are among the most vulnerable road users, and you should always slow down when driving in an area where there is a lot of pedestrian traffic. You should be especially alert to the safety of small children – for example, if you're driving near schools. You also need to watch out for elderly people who might not always manage to cross the road before the traffic lights change.

Most rural roads do not have footpaths and pedestrians have to walk on the margin of the road, however unsuitable that might be. For example, in wet weather the road margin might be very soft or muddy underfoot. Slow down if you see pedestrians on the side of the road ahead – don't expect them to move into the ditch. And be careful not to splash them as you pass.

> You can expect to find higher numbers of pedestrians:
> - At and near bus stops;
> - At the entrances to railway stations;
> - Near schools at opening and closing times;
> - Around sports venues;
> - Along popular jogging routes;
> - Near hospitals; and
> - On shopping streets.

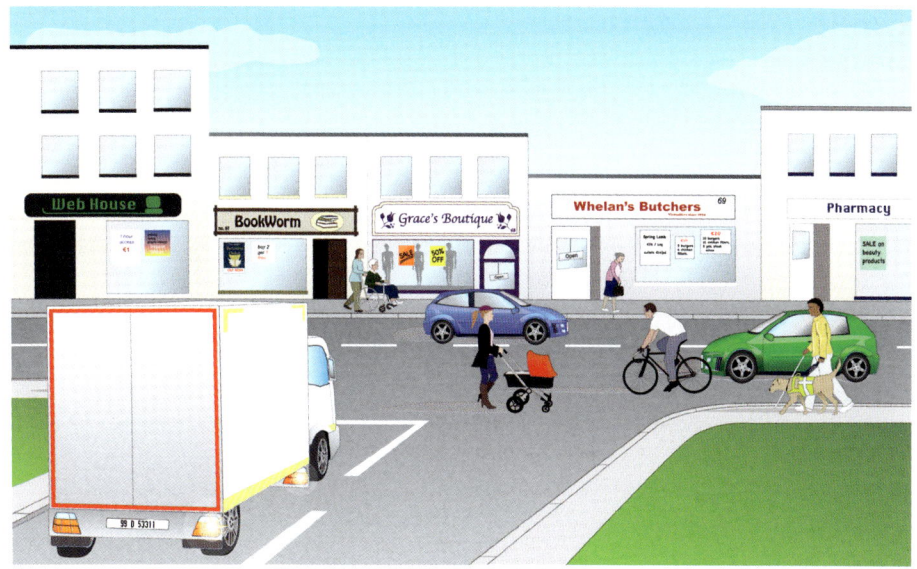

Joining a main road

If you are joining a main road from a side road you should give way to pedestrians on the main road who are crossing the side road.

If you are emerging from a private entrance, you should give way to pedestrians on the margin of the road or on the footpath (if there is one).

Vulnerable road users

Watch out for disabled people and other vulnerable road users – including blind and visually impaired pedestrians (with or without guide dogs). Keep in mind that pedestrians who are deaf or hard of hearing might not hear you coming.

Be careful when passing drivers of powered wheelchairs or other vehicles used by people with disabilities.

Údarás Um Shábháilteacht Ar Bhóithre
Road Safety Authority

Cyclists

Cyclists are just as entitled to use the road as you are, and you need to pay special attention to them.

- Cyclists can sometimes make sudden movements – for example, to avoid a pothole or some broken glass or other objects on the road.
- In bad weather cyclists have less control – they can be blown off balance by strong winds, and they can find it difficult to see in heavy rain. Also they could skid very easily in icy conditions.
- At night, cyclists are more difficult for drivers to see. Even if they have good lights and reflective clothing, cyclists can get 'lost' in the glare of much stronger vehicle lights.
- When you are passing a cyclist, make sure you leave enough room between your truck and the cyclist. The faster you are travelling, the more space you should leave. Avoid passing a cyclist if the road is too narrow – slow down and wait for a wider stretch of road.
- Check your blind spots for cyclists when you manoeuvre in traffic, especially before you pull out into traffic from a parking space.
- If you are turning left, you should give way to cyclists on your inside who are going straight on or turning left. This applies whether or not there is a marked cycle lane. This also applies on roundabouts where you should not cut across a cyclist to make your exit.
- Avoid driving or parking on a cycle lane.
- Be particularly careful dealing with children on bicycles, as they might not have very good road sense or control of their bicycles.
- If traffic is moving slowly, cyclists may overtake you on the inside. Always check your mirrors and your blind spots before turning, changing lane or pulling into the kerb.
- Make sure you use your mirrors before, during and after overtaking a cyclist.

Motorcyclists

Many of the things that you need to keep in mind for cyclists also apply to motorcyclists. Like cyclists, they are also very vulnerable and can easily become 'hidden' in a blind spot or behind a larger vehicle or other obstacles. Because they travel so much faster than cyclists, dangerous situations can arise much more quickly.

- Always look out for motorcyclists when you are emerging from a parking space or a private entrance.
- Due to its small size, a motorcycle may seem further away than it actually is, and it may be difficult to judge its speed.
- Keep your distance when travelling behind a motorcycle.
- Watch out for motorcyclists riding between lanes in slow-moving traffic.

My commitment: 27
I will treat all other road users with courtesy and respect, particularly more vulnerable road users such as pedestrians, cyclists and motorcyclists.
Signed (Learner)

Farm traffic

In rural areas you can expect to meet tractors and other slow-moving agricultural machinery, as well as animals being herded along the road.

- Be patient if you are behind a tractor or other slow-moving agricultural vehicle and cannot pass.
- Slow down if you meet animals being herded along the road or if you meet people on horseback. Don't use your horn, as this might frighten the animals.

In more remote areas of open countryside, you might meet sheep on the road or grazing along the roadside. Slow down until you have passed them, as they are easily frightened and not always predictable in their movements.

Trucks and buses

As a truck driver yourself, you know that driving a large vehicle is not an easy job, especially on some of our narrower urban streets and regional roads. You can help make your fellow truck and bus drivers' jobs a little easier if you take the following into account.

Blind spots	All vehicles have some blind spots, and the bigger the vehicle the bigger the blind spots are. If you are driving behind another truck and you cannot see the truck's mirror, then the truck driver cannot see you.
Turning room	Trucks and buses usually need to swing quite wide to the right before they make a left turn.
Reversing	Trucks and buses sometimes have to reverse into quite restricted spaces – this is especially true for trucks delivering goods. Don't cross behind a large vehicle while it is reversing.
Bus stops	Passenger buses stop frequently to set down and take on passengers, and you should be careful of pedestrians in the vicinity of bus stops. You should give way to a bus that is signalling its intention to rejoin the stream of traffic.

Thinking of the environment

The motor industry is making substantial efforts to reduce the environmental damage caused by driving. Modern vehicles are generally much more efficient in their use of fuel than older ones, have lower greenhouse gas emissions, and cause less pollution.

As a driver, you can also do quite a lot to reduce your personal carbon footprint and to minimise the impact your driving has on the environment.

Fuel-efficient driving

There are a number of simple steps you can take to make your driving more fuel-efficient, and save you money. Drivers who follow these steps are also safer drivers.

Drive smoothly

For greater fuel efficiency, speed up gradually, slow down gradually, and drive smoothly in as high a gear as possible.

- The faster you accelerate the more fuel you use, and there is very little point in accelerating away from one traffic light only to meet a red light at the next.
- Revving or racing your engine while you wait at traffic lights is a waste of fuel.
- Less stopping and starting is more economical.

Fuel efficiency and emission reduction

There are a number of products available that can help to improve fuel efficiency and reduce the harmful emissions your truck produces; these include:

- Proprietary systems where an additive is stored in a separate tank and used by the engine in a process called 'selective catalytic reduction'; and
- Products that you can add directly to the fuel tank each time you fill up.

Service your truck regularly

Have your truck serviced regularly to ensure that you get the best performance and best fuel efficiency. Simple changes such as replacing clogged air or fuel filters can save fuel consumption by up to ten per cent.

Check your tyre pressure regularly

Check your tyre pressure regularly and make sure that you follow the manufacturer's guidelines. Under-inflated tyres drag more on the road, so your engine has to work harder and uses more fuel. Over-inflating your tyres can be dangerous, as they will then have less grip on the road.

My commitment: 28
I accept that driving has an impact on the environment. I will try to minimise that impact by the way that I drive.
Signed (Learner)

Disposing of vehicle waste

Many of the parts and fluids that your truck uses are regarded as 'hazardous waste' when they come to the end of their usefulness. These parts and fluids include engine oil, brake fluid, transmission fluid, antifreeze fluid, oil filters, batteries and so on.

If you do your own vehicle servicing, make sure that you bring all your waste to a recycling centre or to a specialised hazardous waste recycling company licensed by the Environmental Protection Agency. Disposing of vehicle maintenance waste in any other way is illegal, and very damaging to the environment, and you could be prosecuted.

Disposing of your truck

When a truck comes to the end of its life, it must be disposed of in a controlled manner to ensure that it does not pose any threat to the environment.

There are authorised treatment facilities around the country that are licensed to perform this service without charge. Contact your local authority or a main dealer for your make of truck for further information.

My commitment: 29
I understand the hazardous nature of vehicle waste and will never dispose of any waste except through licensed recycling centres.
Signed (Learner)

Údarás Um Shábháilteacht Ar Bhóithre
Road Safety Authority

Dealing with collisions and emergencies

Arriving at the scene of a collision

If you are the first to arrive at the scene of a collision, there are a number of guidelines you need to follow:

- Stay calm, switch off your engine, apply your handbrake and assess the situation.
- Call the emergency services on 999 or 112. Don't assume that other people at the scene of the collision have already done that. Give the emergency services precise information about the nature of the collision, its location, and how many people you think are injured.
- Warn others about the collision:
  - By turning on your hazard lights;
  - By placing a warning triangle on the road a good distance from the site of the collision; and
  - By any other means you think necessary.
- Do not do anything to endanger your own safety. Make sure you are safe yourself before attending to other people, and put on a hi-vis jacket if you have one. Place coats or rugs over anyone who is injured to keep them warm, but do not give them anything to eat or drink.
- Do not move an injured person, unless there is a real danger of fire or of a vehicle turning over. Do not remove helmets from injured motorcyclists. Do not try to lift a vehicle off an injured person without help.
- If you have time, draw a sketch or take photographs of the collision – these may be useful to the authorities investigating how the collision happened.

If you arrive at the scene of a collision and the emergency services are already there, drive on carefully and do not stop.

Reporting a collision

If you are involved in a collision in which anybody is injured, you must report it to An Garda Síochána, either to a garda at the scene or at a Garda station. If there is no garda at the scene, you must give your personal and vehicle details, including insurance details, to anyone involved in the collision and also to any independent witness who asks for this information.

My commitment: 30
If I am ever the first to arrive at the scene of a collision, I will respond quickly, calmly and responsibly, and will do nothing to further endanger the health or safety of anyone.
Signed (Learner)

Dealing with a breakdown

If your truck develops a problem or breaks down, your first thought must be to ensure your own safety and that of other road users.

- If the truck is still driveable, drive it to a safe place off the road or as close to the left as possible. If you are on a motorway, leave the motorway at the next exit.
- If the truck is not still driveable, pull on to the hard shoulder (where there is one) or as close to the left as possible.

Turn on your hazard lights and (if safe to do so) place a red triangle on the hard shoulder or left margin of the road, far enough back to give following traffic adequate warning. Phone for help.

Depending on the circumstances, you will need to decide whether it is safer to keep any passengers you have on the truck or to move them to a safer place. If the breakdown occurs on a motorway and you decide to evacuate the passengers, make sure that they move behind the crash barriers, up the embankment and as far away from the road as possible.

Dealing with a breakdown in a tunnel

If your truck breaks down and becomes no longer driveable while you are driving in a tunnel, switch on the hazard warning lights, pull over as far to the left as you can and switch off the engine. Use the emergency phone at the emergency station to call for help – these are available at frequent intervals in tunnels. Your mobile phone probably won't work in a tunnel.

Follow any advice that the tunnel operator gives you. Evacuate any passengers through one of the emergency exits if advised to do so.

Dealing with a fire on a truck

If a fire breaks out on your truck, you need to take action very quickly.

1. Stop as soon as you can in a safe place, and turn off the engine.
2. Get any passengers off the truck as quickly as possible and move them to a safe place away from the truck.
3. Call the emergency services on 999 or 112.
4. Tackle the fire with a suitable fire extinguisher, but only if it is safe to do so. Do not put yourself at risk.

Dealing with a fire in a tunnel

If a fire breaks out on your truck while you are driving in a tunnel, switch on the hazard warning lights and if possible, drive to the tunnel exit. If it is not safe or possible to drive to the exit, pull over as far to the left as you can, switch off the engine and evacuate any passengers through one of the emergency exits.

Use the emergency phone to call for help, and follow any advice that the the tunnel operator gives you.

Summary of commitments

My commitment: 1

I understand the responsibility of taking a truck onto the road and of sharing the road with other people. I am ready to take on that personal responsibility and to take ownership of how I learn how to drive a truck.

Signed (Learner)

My commitment: 2

I will not take a truck on the road without first carrying out a walk-around check to identify any visible defects and to make sure that the truck is in a roadworthy condition.

Signed (Learner)

My commitment: 3

I am able to start the truck, drive a few metres and stop the truck in a safe location.

I am able to drive the truck in a safe location and can change gears competently.

Signed (Learner)

My commitment: 4

I am able to drive the truck on the public road in a quiet location in very light traffic.

Signed (Learner)

My commitment: 5

I am able to 'read the road' – to take in the information I need from road markings, regulatory and warning signs, traffic lights, and direction signs.

Signed (Learner)

My commitment: 6

I know how to position my truck on the road: I maintain a safe distance between my truck and the vehicle ahead; I understand how lanes work and can position my truck in the appropriate position at all times while driving.

Signed (Learner)

My commitment: 7

I can safely negotiate all types of road junction – including left and right turns (from major to minor and from minor to major roads), slip roads, junctions with traffic lights, and roundabouts.

Signed (Learner)

My commitment: 8

I know when to signal my intentions to other road users – including when to use direction indicators and the horn.

Signed (Learner)

My commitment: 9

I can interpret other road users' intentions – from the signals they give and also from subtle changes in their behaviour.

Signed (Learner)

My commitment: 10

I have practised reversing the truck, including straight, left and right reversing.

I will always exercise great caution when reversing, and will reverse only when I am sure that there are no obstacles or hazards behind the truck.

Signed (Learner)

My commitment: 11

I am able to manoeuvre the truck very precisely at low speeds in forward and reverse gears.

I have practised parking the truck in a variety of locations.

Signed (Learner)

My commitment: 12

I am able to overtake slower-moving vehicles, and do so only when it is necessary, legal and safe.

Signed (Learner)

My commitment: 13

I am able to coordinate and control precisely the clutch, accelerator and handbrake; and I am able to start the truck safely on a hill – both down-hill and uphill.

Signed (Learner)

My commitment: 14

I will always drive in a safe and responsible manner, and try to anticipate danger.

Signed (Learner)

My commitment: 15

I hold a full truck driving licence, have practised motorway driving and understand the challenges that it presents; and in particular, I appreciate the concentration required to drive for prolonged periods at higher speed. I understand the importance of good route planning in advance of beginning a motorway journey.

Signed (Learner)

My commitment: 16

As a professional truck driver, I appreciate the importance of the regulations relating to drivers' hours and daily and weekly rest.

I will always comply with these regulations – as a contribution both to road safety and to my own health and working conditions.

Signed (Learner)

My commitment: 17

I am competent in the use of a tachograph.

As a professional truck driver, I will maintain correct and up-to-date tachograph records at all times.

Signed (Learner)

My commitment: 18

I have practised driving a truck in heavy traffic. I am confident that I can control the truck, remain patient, and deal with the frustrations of being stuck in traffic.

Signed (Learner)

My commitment: 19

I have practised driving at night on a variety of different roads, urban and rural. I understand the particular dangers of driving at night and will always drive with consideration for other road users.

Signed (Learner)

My commitment: 20

I have practised driving in conditions of poor daytime visibility. I appreciate the importance of seeing and being seen.

Signed (Learner)

My commitment: 21

I appreciate the dangers of driving in snow and ice and I will not make any unnecessary journeys in such conditions. When I do drive in snow and ice I will drive slower, leave more room ahead, and accelerate and brake smoothly and gently.

Signed (Learner)

My commitment: 22

I will always drive through road works with care and consideration, and I will obey the warning signs and any instructions the road workers give me.

Signed (Learner)

My commitment: 23

I have practised driving on urban streets and understand the particular hazards I am likely to come across there. I will always drive within the urban speed limit.

Signed (Learner)

My commitment: 24

I have practised driving on country roads and I understand that visibility might be poor and that the road surfaces might be more uneven than on urban or national roads. While driving on country roads I will be considerate to the needs of farmers and other country dwellers and their animals.

Signed (Learner)

My commitment: 25

I will drive only when I am physically fit to do so.
I will never ever drink and drive.
I will never ever drive while under the influence of drugs (legal or illegal).
As a professional driver, I will always work within the Drivers' Hours rules and take adequate rest.

Signed (Learner)

My commitment: 26

I understand the importance of remaining calm, patient and courteous at all times while driving.

I will not allow myself to be 'provoked' by the behaviour of other road users.

Signed (Learner)

My commitment: 27

I will treat all other road users with courtesy and respect, particularly more vulnerable road users such as pedestrians, cyclists and motorcyclists.

Signed (Learner)

My commitment: 28

I accept that driving has an impact on the environment. I will try to minimise that impact by the way that I drive.

Signed (Learner)

My commitment: 29

I understand the hazardous nature of vehicle waste and will never dispose of any waste except through licensed recycling centres.

Signed (Learner)

My commitment: 30

If I am ever the first to arrive at the scene of a collision, I will respond quickly, calmly and responsibly, and will do nothing to further endanger the health or safety of anyone.

Signed (Learner)